D1523805

I'm totally normal. I think it's obnoxious when people demand limos or bodyguards. I eat at McDonald's or Taco Bell. My parents always taught us to be humble. We're not spoiled.
— Paris Hilton
American heiress

The FingerTip Press

Also Available in the *Tipping Points Digest* Series

You Won't Get Fooled Again: More Than 101 Brilliant Ways to Bust Any Bald-Faced Liar (Even If the Liar is Lying Beside You!) by Conner O'Seanery. Discover the freshest and funniest tips for busting the bald-faced liars in your life — whether the liar is a perfect stranger or the person sharing your bed!

Praise for *You Won't Get Fooled Again*

As you belly laugh your way through You Won't Get Fooled Again, *don't be fooled — it's chock full of information. A fast read, read it on the run, on the jog or on the sit.*

But read it! You'll never be the same again.

— Dr. Marcella Bakur Weiner
Relationship expert and co-author of
Cheaters and *The Love Compatibility Book*

You Won't Get Fooled Again *will stand as one of the funniest books on the subject.*

It serves ... tons of tips, but twists straight-up advice into a hilarious pretzel that makes for a delicious read. — David J. Lieberman, Ph.D.
Author of New York Times bestseller
Never Be Lied To Again

...not a replacement for the polygraph; however, this book is the next best thing. The reading is informative and entertaining, and the humor effectively takes the edge off a very serious question: Have I been lied to? (Hint: you probably have!) — Jack Trimarco, Polygraph expert,
host of Court TV's Fake Out

... a hilariously welcome and useful guide to honing one's personal BS detector. Highly recommended. — Midwest Book Review

With a casual writing style laced with wicked humor ... O'Seanery illustrate[s] and inform[s] on every aspect of lying. — Kimberly Orsborn
Mount Vernon News

Blow Your Bank Wad

Blow Your Bank Wad:
More Than 101 Scandalous Ways to Squander Your Kids' Inheritance

Tad and Alicia Carrier-Boxmüeller

Illustrated by Steve Reed

The FingerTip Press

St. Thomas

The following trademark or brand names are used in this digest: Abercrombie & Kent, Alcor, Aston Martin, Berkshire Hathaway, Blancpain, BMW, Boeing, Brioni, Bugatti, Cadillac, Candy Couture, Capgemini SA, Chanel, Charles Schwab, Chopard, Chuck E. Cheese, Citigroup, De Beers, Dover Saddlery, Dylan's Candy Bar, eBay, EDS Corp., Etch-a-Sketch, Fendi, Ferrari, Ford, Four Seasons, Fred Barton Productions, Gap, Grey Goose, Harrods, Hilton, Heritage Gloves, Honma, Horizon & Co., IKEA, J. C. Penney, Jet Networks, Johnson & Johnson, JPMorgan, Kia, Koenigsegg, Lamborghini, LeBlanc, Liberty Media Corp., Life Gem Memorials, Louis Vuitton, M&M, Manolo Blahnik, Maserati, Merrill Lynch, Microsoft, Mikazuki, Millennium Super Yachts, Mohave Aerospace Ventures, Montblanc, Monopoly, National Association of Home Builders, National Association of Realtors, Neiman Marcus, Neorest, NetJets, Nortel, PAGANI, Parker Brothers, Porche, Quaker Oil, residenSea, Rockport, Rolls-Royce, Rubik's Cube, Runco, Saleen, Scaled Composites, Schwinn, Sentient Jet, SKI Club Australia, SSC, Starbucks, Timex, Toto, Victoria's Secret, Virgin, Wal-Mart and Zuber. The author and publisher have no connection to any of these companies or brand-name products … but we'd like to.

Published in 2007 by
The FingerTip Press
14 Chestnut Street, Suite 104
St. Thomas, ON, Canada N5R 2A7
www.tipsdigest.com

Library and Archives Canada Cataloguing in Publication

Carrier-Boxmüeller, Tad, 1967–
    Blow your bank wad : more than 101 scandalous ways to squander your kids' inheritance / Tad and Alicia Carrier-Boxmüeller; illustrated by Steve Reed.

Includes bibliographical references and index.

ISBN 978-0-9739277-5-7

1. Finance, Personal—Humor. 2. Inheritance and succession—Humor. 3. Estate planning—Humor. 4. Parent and child—Humor. I. Carrier- Boxmüeller, Alicia, 1965– II. Title.

HG179.C293   2007   332.024002'07   C2007-900389-3

Tipping Points Digest titles are available at special discounts when purchased in bulk for premiums or institutional use. For more information, please contact us at the above address or send an e-mail to *sales@tipsdigest.com*.

Editor: Bobbie Jo Reid
Cover and Book Design: 1106 Design

First Edition
Printed and bound in Canada
10 9 8 7 6 5 4 3 2 1

For our parents. Enjoy the SKI-ing.

Nothing strengthens the judgment and quickens the conscience like individual responsibility. Nothing adds such dignity to character as the recognition of one's self-sovereignty; the right to an equal place, everywhere conceded — a place earned by personal merit, not an artificial attainment by inheritance, wealth, family and position.
— Elizabeth Cady Stanton
U.S. suffragist, social reformer & author (1815–1902)

Contents

List of TipBits

The heathen are come into thine inheritance,
And thy temple have they defiled.
— T. S. Eliot
British poet & critic (1888–1965)

Introduction

Right now, as you read this introduction, millions of Baby Boomers are sitting in quaint breakfast nooks all across the continent, rubbing their hands with unbridled glee, laughing maniacally as they contemplate the cash bonanza that will drop into their laps the instant dear ol' Ma and Pa drop dead.

You see, a Mount Everest of money is set to change hands over the next twenty years. North America's Boomers stand to inherit an estimated $10 *trillion* between now and the year 2027, and roughly 90% of this mind-boggling windfall will take place in the United States. Stretch the timeline out to 2052, and the grubby pile of cash transferring from generation to generation grows to a nearly incomprehensible $41 trillion.

To put this tidy sum into perspective, *all* the nations of the world spent a combined $1 trillion on defense in 2004 (47% of which was accounted for by the U.S.'s defense budget). Just imagine what the more belligerent leaders of the world would do to get their hands on a $41 trillion money pot!

Rest assured, the kids of these Baby Boomers have their eyes on the prize as well, waiting with bated breath for their own ship — luxury liner, actually — to come steaming into port. It's still a long way from the shore, but it's on their radar screen.

We want to stop this madness. We want you to *SKI* that mountain of money: *S*pend (the) *K*ids' *I*nheritance. Every thin dime of it.

It's not that we hate children. Like Whitney Houston (a model parent if ever there was one), we believe that children are our future. Heck, we're parents ourselves. Raised a fine daughter from a squealing bundle to a precocious toddler to a sullen teenager to a confident young woman.

Among these milestones, we performed the requisite parental duties: Late-night trips to the emergency room whenever her fever spiked; soul-destroying birthday parties at Chuck E. Cheese (is it just us, or would a mandatory year-long stint as a weekend Chuck E. Cheese employee be a viable alternative to capital punishment in discouraging capital crimes?); spectator time on frigid sidelines during her ill-conceived foray into soccer; graduation ceremonies whose opulence rivaled Prince Charles and Lady Di's wedding (can anyone explain why a primary-school graduation requires a prom dress?); chauffeuring her to her closest friends, who invariably lived on the farthest side of town; and countless additional duties that make parenting the most demanding job on earth.

We did these things willingly, with love. But the one thing we won't do is saddle our daughter with an inheritance. No way, no how. We won't afflict her with "affluenza" or early onset Sudden Wealth Syndrome.

Cruel? Far from it. We simply buy into a philosophy one of the wealthiest industrialists to ever draw breath was selling many years ago:

The parent who leaves his son enormous wealth generally deadens the talents and energies of the son and tempts him to lead a less useful and less worthy life than he otherwise would.
— Andrew Carnegie
U.S. industrialist & philanthropist (1835–1919)

Gender bias aside, Carnegie knew what he was talking about. You can't amass a $100 billion fortune (in today's dollars) and not know your way around a campfire. Carnegie recognized the damage to a child's motivation that would be wrought by a windfall inheritance.

Now, you probably don't have anywhere near $100 billion earmarked for your kids, but that's beside the point. It doesn't matter whether you have a small fortune or small change in the bank. It doesn't matter if you can't tell a T-Bill from a T-bone. What matters is that you spend your hard-earned money on yourself before you depart this life.

....

TipBit: How Does Your Estate Rate?

A 2006 *New York Times* survey of estates delved deep to answer the following question: How much is the average American estate worth? Put another, more self-centered way: How much cash will I get my hands on when my folks cash in their chips?

Here's what the *Times* uncovered:

❖ The upper 2% of all U.S. estates are worth at least $782,300

❖ The next 3% are priced between $326,000 and $782,300

❖ The next 5% amount to between $244,600 and $326,000

This upper 10% of all American households — the elite — pulls the purse strings on the vast majority of the nation's private wealth.

> And what about the riffraff adrift in the remaining 90%?
> ❖ The next 40% of American estates can scratch together between $52,200 and $244,600
> ❖ The next 20% can cough up between $2,600 and $52,200
> ❖ The bottom 30% are worth less than $2,600
>
> While these numbers indicate an inheritance won't be a life-changing lottery win for most Americans, they don't stop most Americans from dreaming about cashing in and telling their boss to stick this job up his kilt.

Don't think you need to be a grisly geriatric with one foot in the grave and another on a banana peel to benefit from this philosophy. Just like it's never too early to start saving for retirement, it's never too early to start spending your kids' inheritance. That's where this digest comes in.

Blow Your Bank Wad will open your eyes to the mouth-watering possibilities unfettered SKI-ing unlocks. We've scoured the world, leaving no gemstone unturned, to assemble the most scandalous ways to poach your nest egg. In the chapters that follow, you'll learn why spending your kids' inheritance is actually the *best thing* you can do for them. You'll discover wicked ways to upgrade you home, your cars, your boats, your planes, your travels, your "bling" and your life. And along the way, you'll encounter the funniest, most fascinating and most frightening aspects of inheritance, estate planning and unbridled indulgence.

So, whether you're the parents of a Boomer, or a Boomer with grown children of your own or a young couple with a tyke who's about to experience her first Chuck E. Cheese party (our deepest sympathies), this digest is for you.

Go forth and SKI that mountain of money.

— Tad and Alicia Carrier-Boxmüeller

Everywhere You Want to Be, April 2007

Vulgar Word Alert!

As a service to our faithful readers around the world — and to the governments whose arbitrary fiddling with customs duties could erase our already slender profit margin — The FingerTip Press reserves this space in every *Tipping Points Digest* for Vulgar Word Alerts.

While no digest published by The FingerTip Press would dare touch the Holy Trinity of swear words with a 10-foot type-writer ribbon, certain works may contain potentially offensive words, sentences or paragraphs (or entire chapters if they refer in any way to the National Hockey League's '04–'05 season). Our Vulgar Word Alert! service is designed to safeguard you, the reader, and your loved ones from potential trauma. Think of this service as the literary equivalent of the FCC's five-second delay for live-television broadcasts.

Blow Your Bank Wad features salty or suggestive language on the following pages: 35, 41, 46, 51, 70, 72, 79, 91 and 99.

Parents of impressionable ankle-biters are advised to either:

1. Strike the offensive word(s) using black, indelible marker;

2. Tear out the offensive page(s) and shred along with your bank statements and the unpublished novel you've been working on for eight years; or

3. Stash the digest in the same place you hide your "artistic" late-night material.

Remember: Forewarned is forearmed.

The Men, Women and Children of The FingerTip Press

Chapter 1

The Kids Are Alright
(Unless You Ruin Them with Money)

I would as soon leave my son a curse as the almighty dollar.
— Andrew Carnegie

Just for the sake of argument, we'll assume you're having trouble coming to grips with the notion of spending your kids' inheritance. Leaving the whole "love" issue aside for the moment, there's a moral or ethical wall against which the SKI-ing philosophy butts. We can imagine the incredulous thoughts zipping through your head:

"Spend my kids' inheritance? Are you crazy? How callous and unfeeling do you think I am?"

Relax. No one is questioning your love for your children. But the blinding emotional quotient of SKI-ing makes it impossible to see its primary benefit: Spending your kids' inheritance is, in fact, better for the kids.

TipBit: Inheritance is Going to the Dogs

When Eleanor Ritchey, the unmarried Quaker Oil heiress, died in 1968, she left her entire $4.2 million fortune to

150 homeless dogs she had adopted over the years. Ritchey's relatives contested the will, but the dogs — and their lawyer — carried the day. The dogs retired in style on a 180-acre ranch in Deerfield Beach, Florida.

No word on where their lawyer retired.

Would it surprise you to know that one-third of affluent Americans already embrace the SKI-ing philosophy? A recent survey commissioned by financial-services company Charles Schwab found 33% of affluent Americans age 45 and older believe it's better to spend their money in their lifetime. If you are part of this group, you have our permission to skip this chapter and proceed directly to the fun stuff in Chapter 2.

If you are part of the 66% who need convincing, however, keep reading. This chapter will help reduce the emotional glare so you can clearly spot the logic of spending your kids' inheritance.

What's Love Got to Do With It?

Let's put the "love" issue to bed right from the get-go. Like most parents, your gut reaction to blowing your bank wad — rather than hoarding and bequeathing it to your children when you die — is probably indigestion. The notion tastes cold and bitter, reducing your love for your kids to a thin gruel only Scrooge could enjoy.

Nonsense. You're thinking with your heart, not your head. Stop castigating yourself and consider this: You've spent virtually every second as a parent focusing on nothing *but* your children. *Their* safety. *Their* comfort. *Their* welfare. *Their* happiness. Sure, you've slipped some me-time into the mix, just to stop yourself from plowing your SUV through a crowd of people. But, on average, your welfare has finished a distant second to that of your kids. It's time for *you* to finish first for once.

What's more, you've already sunk a tractor-trailer load of cash into your kids. According to the U.S. Department of Agriculture's 2005 annual report, "Expenditures on Children by Families," the average couple earning $43,200 to $72,600 in pre-tax income spends $190,980 raising a child to age 17. Based on an average family size of 1.8 children, that's an investment of nearly $350,000 for most couples. And that's assuming you stop spending money on your children when they turn 17. Raise your hand if any of your brood has moved — or is planning to move — out of the house at that tender age. Kids today need to be levered out of the house in

their mid-30s. As the movie *Failure to Launch* aptly illustrated, it sometimes takes a crowbar shaped like Sarah Jessica Parker.

Place your rational investor's hat on your head and pretend you're pumping money into a fledgling business called MyKids, Inc. By the time MyKids, Inc. celebrates its twenty-first year of operation, your rounds of financing should be finished. Every business eventually has to stand on its own two feet (unless, of course, it's run by the government). Continue to finance your kids after they reach adulthood and you risk turning them into a government corporation, with all its attendant qualities: bloated, non-competitive, grossly inefficient and characterized by an alarming sense of expectation and entitlement.

Far from being callous or unloving, spending your kids' inheritance has all the earmarks of sound parenting. In our humble opinion, preventing your children from becoming living, breathing versions of the Department of Motor Vehicles is the finest expression of love you can offer.

....
TipBit: A Caveat for Lending Money
Nothing in the SKI-ing philosophy says you can't *lend* your children money. If you want to give them a step up by giving them, say, a down payment for a house, go for it. Just don't *give* them the money. Make it a loan, with the requisite documentation and repayment terms. Be as generous with the terms as you like, but not so generous that you'll be chewing dandelion roots before it's repaid.
....

The Deadly Disease Known as Affluenza

The affliction of affluenza carries the following symptoms: deadening of spirit, softening of motivation and weakening of resolve to carve one's own niche in life. Affluenza also carries the potential for scrambling the intellect, if America's most famous heiress is any example:

> *It's traditional for an heiress to be raised in a sheltered way.*
> *No one thinks this is true of me, but it actually was.*
> — Paris Hilton
> Like you don't know who she is

Hilton's comment, though laughable considering her forays into reality television and Internet sexcapades, does contain a solemn truth. Wealth can isolate people. And nothing isolates people as readily or completely as inherited wealth. Look no farther than the documentary *Born Rich* for proof of this truism. In fact, make this film your next stop in your field research on the drawbacks of inheritance.

Born Rich is a 2003 documentary by Jamie Johnson, a Johnson & Johnson heir. Rather than remain idly rich in his early adulthood, Johnson — against the wishes of his family and advice of his lawyer — decided to document the lifestyle of his closest friends, who happen to be the children of America's richest families. The resulting 60 minutes of film provides a fascinating glimpse into a world few inhabit. After its viewing, you'll thank your lucky stars it's a world your children will never inhabit.

What makes *Born Rich* remarkable is Johnson's ability to extract frank and open discussion on the effects of wealth from the members of this notoriously private club. The documentary's cast of characters reads like a Who's Who of the MTV generation's social register: Donald Trump's daughter, Ivanka (who opines at one point that her dad had it worse than homeless people because he was once billions of dollars in debt); S. I. Newhouse IV, heir to the Condé Nast publishing empire (who, despite a net worth equal to Spain's Gross National Product, can't afford a proper first name); Josiah Hornblower, a Whitney/Vanderbilt heir; Georgina Bloomberg, daughter of New York's mayor; and others.

The cast members — each one of them — come off as a species of rare bird, ensconced in gilded cages purchased with fortunes they had no hand in amassing. Inheriting at 21 years of age more money than can be spent in a lifetime has erased their need to work, eliminating the driving force that motivates 99.9% of North Americans to get out of bed five or six or seven days a week. Johnson himself neatly captures the morass when he observes how he lives "outside the American dream." The hunger to make his mark and build his fortune was satisfied decades before he was even born.

··

TipBit: Working for the Weekend

To be fair, some members of the elite club featured in *Born Rich* have looked for meaningful paid employment to augment their titanic trust funds. Stephanie Ercklentz, a self-admitted shopaholic, thought about becoming a doctor, but decided it would be too demanding. She also worked for a short period as an investment banker, but the long hours on Wall Street cut into her Bellini time with her buddies.

Georgina Bloomberg has put her multi-million-dollar stamp on the equestrian world, winning numerous championships. She's earned hundreds of thousands from sponsorships by Dover Saddlery and Heritage Gloves, and is touted as a contender to represent the U.S. at the 2008 Olympics. Nice to see she isn't simply buying the gold medal.

In the end, the members of this exclusive — and involuntary — club are left to find some meaningful niche to call their own. Tellingly, all possess a modicum of awareness that a life devoted entirely to leisure is a dangerous quagmire; nearly every family can rhyme off examples of drug addiction or abject misery stemming from a lack of purpose.

By the time the credits roll on *Born Rich*, you'll be left feeling sorry for these children, confined as they are to trot the same laps around the same circle of friends, never able to freely discuss their troubles with outsiders because — let's face it — what outsider could possibly sympathize? Your children shouldn't suffer the same isolating fate, and they won't once you embrace the SKI-ing philosophy.

TipBit: Wash the Floors, Cinderella, Do the Dishes, Cinderella

Upper-income Americans are so determined the "habits of industry" not be lost on their children that 99% of rich kids are made to tidy their rooms, 85% to take out the trash and 77% and 81%, respectively, to take part-time jobs while in high school or at college, according to a survey by

U.S. Trust. Now that you mention it, we could use some help around our place. Wonder if they do windows, too?

Even the Super-Rich are SKI-ing

In 2006, the number of billionaires in the world grew to 793, up from 691 the year before, according to *Forbes*. Favorable economic conditions raised all the boats in the ultra-rich harbor; the net worth of the billionaires' club increased 18% from 2005 to $2.6 trillion. Here's a snapshot of the list's top three members, just in case you're trolling for a loan to re-sod your lawn:

No. 1: Bill Gates topped the *Forbes* list for the twelfth straight year. His net worth of $50 billion still isn't enough to buy a decent haircut, though.

No. 2: Snapping at Gates' heels is investor Warren Buffett, CEO of Berkshire Hathaway, who has tucked away $42 billion. He may have dropped a notch or two, however, following his donation of over $30 billion to the William and Melinda Gates Foundation in the summer of 2006.

No. 3: Rapidly climbing the billionaire ladder on rungs made of high-speed telephone cable is Carlos Slim Helu, the Mexican telecom mogul. He's put $30 billion into the vault.

TipBit: The Rollback Windfall

Curious to know where your Wal-Mart Rollback savings are going? Five members of the Walton family occupied spots 17 through 21 on the 2006 *Forbes* list, with Christy Walton (widow of John Walton, who died in 2005 when his ultra-light aircraft crashed) and Jim Walton tied for No. 17 with $15.9 billion each. The combined wealth of Sam Walton's progeny totals nearly $79 billion.

Now you know why the Wal-Mart smiley face is smiling.

There's a trend afoot among the world's ultra-wealthy, however. The richest of the rich are ridding themselves of their fortunes, choosing to divest the lion's share of their loot on philanthropic causes, rather than the kiddiewinks. Bill Gates established the William and Melinda Gates Foundation in 2000, which focuses on global health issues and improving U.S. libraries and high schools. Like a latter-day Andrew Carnegie, he has vowed to give away most of his fortune before he dies.

Jumping into the philanthropy ring in a major way in 2006 was Warren Buffett, who attracted international attention with a $30 billion gift to the Gates Foundation. Buffett has pledged to annually donate 5% of his stock holdings, so long as Bill or Melinda plays an active role with the foundation. Thanks to Buffett's lift, the Gates Foundation's total endowment is $60 billion, five times that of the next largest U.S. charity: The Ford Foundation. (How much do you want to bet Ford Motor Company's executives are burning the midnight oil, trying to come up with a legal way to tap into the foundation's $11.5 billion worth of assets in order to prop up the company's sagging bottom line?)

Expect anti-trust investigators to stick their noses in any day now, given this blatant attempt by Gates and Buffett to monopolize the philanthropy market. Also expect to receive a computer virus instead of a tax receipt every time you make a $10 donation.

TipBit: O.K., It's Not Really a Monopoly

With the addition of Buffett's $30 billion, the Gates Foundation will be capable of doling out roughly $3 billion a year. While that's a hefty sum, it represents only a smidge over 1% of the $260.3 billion in charitable contributions given by generous Americans in 2005. None of which came our way, by the way. Thanks, America.

In September 2006, Sir Richard Branson — renowned adventurer and chairman of the Virgin Group — announced at the Bill Clinton Global Initiative in New York that all profits from his airline and rail businesses over the next 10 years would be directed to combating global warming. The sum is expected to exceed $3 billion.

Al Gore, former U.S. vice president and star of the sleeper hit *An Inconvenient Truth,* evidently played a pivotal role in Sir Richard's decision. "Al Gore came to my home in London," Branson remarked at the New York conference, "and said, 'You are in a position to make a difference, and if you make a giant step forward, others will follow.'"

Now it makes sense. We're willing to bet most people would gladly fork over $3 billion if it got Al Gore to stop talking and leave their homes.

....
TipBit: George Lucas' Largesse
Star Wars creator George Lucas announced in September 2006 that his private foundation would gift $175 million to his alma mater, the University of Southern California. What he failed to mention, however, was that $174.5 million of the gift was, in fact, punitive damages for introducing Jar Jar Binks in *Star Wars Episode I: The Phantom Menace.*
....

One More Time ... With Feeling

Still with us? Great! That means we've at least partially shaded your mind from the glaring emotional quotient of the SKI-ing philosophy. Enough to get you this far, anyway. And now that you're here, please allow us one more hit of the hammer. Repeat the following mantra until it's etched into your brain — or until your children refer you to a psychiatrist:

Embracing the SKI-ing philosophy makes perfect sense because:

❖ It lets your kids do life's heavy lifting, which strengthens their character and fully develops their potential.

❖ You've already invested a hefty sum in their upbringing. It's time to invest in *you*.

❖ It removes any possibility of them contracting affluenza — and suffering through life with its debilitating effects.

❖ There are better ways to spend your money. As the über-rich demonstrate, philanthropy is a viable alternative — and it might just get your name on a hospital wing.

If philanthropy isn't your cup of karma, however, don't sweat it. The chapters that follow will provide plenty of mind-blowing possibilities for blowing your bank wad. From your home to your vehicles to your travels to your bling, the remainder of this digest will help expand your mind and shrink your net worth.

··

TipBit: Brooke Astor is Broke

Here's a cautionary tale that exemplifies why bequeathing your fortune to your kids might not be the best strategy. Brooke Astor is 104 years old and lives on porridge and peas in a rundown New York apartment. On the best of days, this should spark outrage. But the tale is made even more infuriating considering Brooke Astor is the widow of Vincent Astor, son of John Jacob Astor IV (who perished on the *Titanic* in 1912), and inherited a $45 million fortune from her late husband.

How can a 104-year-old woman worth $45 million be living in squalor, you ask? Her fortune is controlled by her son and legal guardian, Anthony Marshall, we answer.

Marshall's own son, Philip, has accused his father of keeping Brooke Astor in the poorhouse in order to feather his own nest. Anthony Marshall, you see, receives $2.3 million a year to control his mother's money. Philip alleges the following misdeeds on the part of his deadbeat dad:

❖ Despite his mother's occasional falls from her bed, Anthony has refused to buy her a hospital bed fitted with railings.

❖ Anthony has denied his mother's frequent requests for non-skid socks.

❖ Anthony replaced his mother's French chef with a variety-challenged cook who serves up a putrid diet of puréed peas, carrots, liver and oatmeal.

❖ Anthony has eliminated his mother's supply of hair dye and beloved cosmetics.

These accusations have yet to be proven in court. Philip wants his father replaced as his grandmother's legal guardian by Annette de la Renta, wife of fashion mogul Oscar. Should the allegations prove true, we can think of only one word to describe Anthony Marshall. Unfortunately, we can't print it here.

....

The worst thing you can do is to take away a kid's ambition.
That's what can happen with money.
— Ken Thomson
Media baron & late patriarch of Canada's wealthiest family (1923–2006)

Chapter 2

Home, Sprawling Home

*But a cultivated man becomes ashamed of his property,
out of new respect for his nature. Especially he hates what he
has if he sees that it is accidental, came to him by inheritance,
or gift, or crime; then he feels that it is not having;
it does not belong to him, has no root in him ...*
— Ralph Waldo Emerson, "Self-Reliance," *Essays*
U.S. essayist, poet & philosopher (1803–1882)

It's your castle, your fortress of solitude and your refuge from the raging storms of the world. It likely represents your biggest investment, unless you dumped a ton of money into Nortel stock in the late '90s (the value of which is now exceeded by the comic books gathering dust in your basement). It's your home.

If experience is any guide, you've sunk thousands into making your home a safe environment for your kids. Childproof electrical outlets, cupboards and drawers. Asbestos removal for those lucky buyers who purchased charming character homes with high ceilings and crown moldings fashioned from unidentifiable wood. ("It's oak. No, it's cherrywood. No, it's sycamore.") A second deadbolt on every door to prevent your recently exiled teenager from sneaking back into the house and cleaning out the liquor cabinet while you're away. (Technically, that's making your home a safe environment *from* your kids.)

....

TipBit: Dust in the Windfall

You might want to dust the cobwebs off that pile of comic books in the basement. In 2006, Tom Crippen faced the depressing task of clearing the junk out of his late father's New York home. Davis Crippen, Tom's father, was an incorrigible packrat. True to form, his basement was packed to the rafters with debris. Among the clutter, however, Tom discovered a collection of 11,000 comic books, the culmination of a lifetime hobby his father had started when he was a wee lad in short pants. Many of the titles date from the late '30s to the mid-'50s — the Golden Age of comics — which spawned the likes of Superman, Batman and the Flash.

They didn't call it the Golden Age for nothin'; appraisers valued the collection at $2.5 million. Heritage Auction Galleries of Dallas, Texas sold the first batch of 550 comics in August 2006, netting Tom, his mother and brother $717,000.

We think that's super, man.

....

Dwarfing the money spent on making your home safe for your kids, however, is the money spent on fixing the damage caused by your kids over the years. Here's a snapshot of some of the wear and tear we've encountered:

❖ Grape soda spilled on a two-day-old sofa upholstered in cream Italian silk.

❖ Herringbone oak hardwood floor reduced to an Etch-a-Sketch pad by the hard, rubber wheels of toy trucks, tricycles, in-line skates, etc.

❖ VCR choked to death by insertion of grilled-cheese sandwich (this back when you needed a second mortgage to buy a VCR).

❖ Fridge door ripped from its hinges when its interior shelves were used as a set of climbers on a rainy Sunday afternoon.

❖ Drywall in bedroom "accidentally" caved in by a blunt object following a grounding-the-daughter incident.

❖ Carpeting, linoleum, washer and dryer, computer, six interior walls, doghouse, dog and barbeque destroyed or stolen during a party that spontaneously erupted during the first — and last — weekend we left our teenager home alone.

These items can add up to big money over 21 years. The beauty of the SKI-ing philosophy, however, is that it permits you to start sinking money into your home on *your* terms. Emancipated from the obligation to tuck every dollar away for your kids, you can focus on creating the kind of palace you've always dreamed about.

TipBit: Buffett Says "Stuff It" to Selling

According to the National Association of Realtors, roughly one-fifth of a household's wealth is composed of home equity. Imagine if that ratio held true for Warren Buffett, CEO of Berkshire Hathaway and the second richest man in the world. His estimated net worth of $42 billion would translate into a property worth $8.4 billion. Buffett, however, has sunk considerably less than 20% of his net worth into his digs. In fact, the pre-eminent buy-and-hold investor has owned the same Omaha home he purchased for $31,500 nearly 50 years ago. Like so many of Buffett's investments, it's appreciated a fair bit over time; in 2003, a local assessor pegged its value at nearly $700,000. Buffett, by the way, thought the figure overvalued the property by $200,000.

Because this is unfamiliar territory for most parents — especially those with new homes (or new mortgages, anyway) and even newer children — the remainder of this chapter provides a glimpse inside the architecture of the possible, made possible when you embrace the SKI-ing philosophy.

A Home to Call Your Own

The National Association of Home Builders tells us the median American house size weighs in at slightly more than 2,000 square feet. Inside the average home are three bedrooms and a fireplace, and the whole package is tastefully wrapped in vinyl or aluminum siding. We want to expand your mind, though, so let's examine some places that stretch these numbers beyond the breaking point.

Microsoft Fortune Leads to Macro-sized Home

A good starting point is the home of the world's richest man. Microsoft founder Bill Gates' Medina, Washington home is more than 25 times the average size. Let's take a magical mystery tour of this magnificent property ... by the numbers. Match the following statements on the left to the correct answers on the right. (But don't you dare write in this book!) Check the answer key — and your Gates Quotient — on page 20.

1. Number of handles per door, each custom-machined to Mr. Gates' specifications.

   A. 2

2. Price, in U.S. dollars, of each custom-machined door handle.

   B. 6

3. Dimensions, in feet, of the swimming pool, which is fitted with an underwater music system.

   C. 7

4. Miles of communication cable in the home.

   D. 8

5. Number of bedrooms, according to the property records.

   E. 17 by 60

6. Price, in U.S. dollars, Gates paid for the lot in December 1988.

   F. 42

7. Annual property tax, in U.S. dollars.

   G. 53

8. Number of square feet the main house occupies.

   H. 104

9. Weight, in pounds, of some of the home's interior doors. (Considering Bill's brawn, it's a good thing they're perfectly balanced for easy use.)

   I. 800

10. Number of inches within which the sensors   **J.** 2,000
embedded in the floor can track a visitor.
(No sneaking into Bill's bedroom to see
what kind of underwear he likes!)

11. Weight, in pounds, of the granite slab that   **K.** 4,500
serves as a shower curtain beside the spa.

12. Linear feet of hanging space in Melinda's   **L.** 50,000
closet for her clothes.

13. Number of electricians who were working   **M.** 990,000
on the house at one point during construction.

14. Price, in U.S. dollars, Gates paid for the   **N.** 2,000,000
Codex Leicester, Leonardo da Vinci's
handwritten folio of scientific observations
and illustrations on natural phenomena.
(Look for it the home's main library next
time you're over for coffee and sticky buns.
Just don't get any on the Codex!)

15. Number of years it took to build the house.   **O.** 30,800,000

Answer Key:

1. A	6. N	11. K
2. J	7. M	12. F
3. E	8. L	13. H
4. G	9. I	14. O
5. D	10. B	15. C

Rate Your Gates Quotient

0–5 correct: Your knowledge of all things Gates sucks. Stop sucking!

6–10 correct: You demonstrate a solid working knowledge of the world's richest man. Celebrate by vacuuming your computer keyboard.

11–15 correct: Your score suggests an obsessive compulsion. Please visit *www.microsoft.com* to download your restraining order.

TipBit: U.S. Estate Tax — Part I

Searching for a scapegoat on whom to blame high estate taxes? Look no farther than U.S. president Franklin D. Roosevelt. He introduced the estate tax in the U.S. Congress in 1935. Roosevelt invoked the ghost of Andrew Carnegie, who once observed "where wealth accrues honorably, the people are always silent partners." Just as Roosevelt believed inherited political power was inconsistent with political equality, he was convinced inherited wealth was inconsistent with social equality.

Steel Yourself for Sticker Shock

Lakshmi Mittal, Indian steel baron and fifth-richest man on the planet, set a worldwide price record for a private home in 2004 when he plunked down $128 million for his 12-bedroom townhouse in London's chi-chi Kensington Palace Gardens. A stone's throw from the royal family's Kensington Palace, the property comprises the former Egyptian and Russian embassies

and covers 55,000 square feet. Found somewhere inside this mammoth home is a ballroom, Turkish baths, a 20-car garage and a swimming pool inlaid with precious gems.

....

TipBit: "What Do You Mean, Cash Bar?"

In 2005, just to prove the purchase of the world's most expensive private home didn't set him too far back, Lakshmi Mittal forked out $60 million for his 23-year-old daughter Vanisha's wedding. He chartered 12 Boeing jets to fly 1,500 guests from India for five days of fun and trivolity in France (Vanisha was married in a charming seventeenth-century chateau). Prior to this epic example of wedding planning, however, he delivered silver-encased invitations 20 pages thick containing jade necklaces or diamond watches to close family friends. (George Costanza this guy is not!)

One thousand guests stayed in a five-star hotel in Paris on Mittal's nickel during the five-day lootapalooza, which also featured a performance by Aussie chanteuse, Kylie Minogue. We're guessing her appearance fee was the cheapest part of the nuptials.

....

Rooms to Spare

Prince Alwaleed bin Talal Alsaud of Saudi Arabia, No. 8 on the *Forbes* billionaire list, has a 317-room palace in Riyadh, which cost $130 million to build. Totaling a mind-numbing 400,000 square feet, it has a soccer field (inside the home?), eight elevators and more than 500 television sets. Then again, with $20 billion in the bank, he can probably afford the cable bill.

IKEA: "I Know *Eeets* Affordable."

As outlandish as their homes may be, some of the world's wealthiest men and women have decidedly downscaled digs that wouldn't be out of place in the most modest neighborhoods. Ingvar Kamprad, founder and former chief executive of IKEA, may hold the No. 4 spot on the *Forbes* list, but he's also an infamous penny-pincher who rattles around town in a second-hand Volvo. His house in Lausanne, Switzerland, is said to be surprisingly unremarkable, despite Kamprad's net worth of $28 billion.

Let's Check the Real Estate Listings

There's no need to build a palatial home from scratch when there's plenty to buy on the open market. Here are four fantastic properties that would do any upwardly mobile SKI-er proud:

Updown Court Is Upscale to the Max

Updown Court in Surrey, England is billed as the world's most expensive home. Priced at over $130 million when it went up for sale in February 2005, the 103-room estate boasts more living space than the royal residences of Hampton Court and Buckingham Palace combined.

Updown Court is actually made up of four principal buildings: the main house, guest accommodation, a gate lodge and a separate estate manager's office. (You can't be expected to run a place this big on your own!) For the dads in the studio audience accustomed to sharing a single bathroom with the wife and kids, this little piece of heaven features 22 bedroom/bathroom suites. For the fashionistas in the studio audience, the main house's entrance has a sweeping double staircase identical to the one found in the late Gianni Versace's Miami home. And for the paranoid types in the studio audience, the main house also contains a panic room, just in case terrorists — or Jodie Foster — drop by for a dip in one of the estate's five swimming pools.

Lesley Allen-Vervcoe, the developer who acquired the property in 1987 after it was partially destroyed by fire, has added a slew of upgrades every home buyer desires: a helipad, a heated marble driveway, a 50-seat theatre, an underground garage big enough to accommodate eight limousines (and the egos of their occupants) and a study featuring a mosaic floor detailed with 24-karat gold leafing.

Better have deep pockets if you're hoping to close escrow on Updown Court; the maximum loan for a property in England is roughly $47 million.

Take a peek at what $130 million gets you at *www.updown court.com*

....

TipBit: Cash and Carry the Mortgage

A recent survey of upscale mortgage brokers by *Unique Homes* magazine found that 54% of home buyers who part with $1,000,000 or more for their properties pay cash. Many of these buyers cite privacy protection as the main reason. No word on how many sprinkle their speech with the phrase "*Fuhgeddaboutit!*" while haggling over the price.

....

Trump Trumps Them All

The most expensive home in America is owned by none other than Donald Trump. The *Maison de l'Amité* (House of

Friendship) is an oceanfront estate located in Palm Beach, Florida. Trump purchased the place for $41.35 million and set Kendra Todd, one of his *Apprentice* winners, to work on a massive reno. We're talking Ty Pennington on steroids and crystal meth, without the gut-wrenching pathos.

Twelve bedrooms were added to the estate, bringing the total to 15, and the property now sports a cut-coral façade, an eight-car garage, an observatory and an "unfurnished" 33,000-square-foot lower level that a prospective buyer can appoint to his or her taste. You have to wonder what could possibly fill this space. An aircraft hangar? A Costco warehouse? A grow-op big enough to supply the entire eastern seaboard with "medicinal" marijuana?

Oh, want to know the value of the remodeled digs? An astounding $125 million. But if fixtures and drapes aren't included, it's no deal!

Three Ponds for $25 Million Apiece

The second-most-expensive home in the U.S. is the breathtaking Three Ponds Farm Estate of Bridgehampton, New York. The 25,000-square-foot house, designed by Allan Greenberg, is built to the highest standards, but it's the extras that really pump up the price. Three Ponds encompasses 60 acres of rolling waterfront farmland, with a U.S. Golf Association-rated golf course and pro shop occupying 25 of the 60 acres. The estate's ponds are stocked with bass, perch and pickerel, and there's a grass tennis court where you can work out the kinks after a hard day of hooking golf balls and fish. Asking price? $75 million.

Pent Up in the Pierre's Penthouse

If you're willing to settle for third, the next-most-expensive home in America is the three-floor penthouse at the famed Pierre Hotel in New York. When it comes to unobstructed views of Central Park, the penthouse at the Pierre can't be beat. When it comes to hefty maintenance fees, the penthouse at the Pierre can't be beat, either. They'll run you $45,000 a month. A drop in the ol' bucket, really, compared to the asking price of $70 million.

TipBit: The Rich Keep Gettin' Richer

As with the Billionaire's Club, the Millionaire's Club has seen its ranks swell in recent years. Boasting over 8.7 million members in 2005, the assets of the world's millionaires increased 8.5% to $33.3 trillion, according to a report published by Capgemini SA and Merrill Lynch. It looks like the upward climb will continue, too; the report forecasted continued asset growth at a rate of 6% per year for the next five years, meaning the total net worth of this select group could surpass $44 *trillion* by 2010.

Seclusion at Its Finest ... and Most Expensive

You know what real estate is all about, right? Location, location and location. If you're looking for a place to get away from it all — or a place where the kids won't be able to track you down after you skip town with their trust fund — it's tough to beat the seclusion offered by a private island. Lucky for you, there's some gems on the market:

Isla de sa Ferradura for a Premium

The Isla de sa Ferradura may offer only 14 acres of living space, but it's worth every penny of the $39.7 million list price. Located a short hop from the northern coast of Ibiza, the resort island sports a luxe hacienda, edged by Harlequin Romance-inspired cliffs and lapping surf. The hacienda itself ain't too shabby, either. It comes with a home theatre, a dining room with elbow room for 14 and a revolving terrace overlooking the pool ... and the pool's waterfall and wet bar. All this luxury is accessible by yacht, helicopter or the private road that links Ferradura to the main island.

Get away from it all on the Isla de sa Ferradura by visiting *www.vladi-private-islands.de*.

Pakatoa Island Packs a Punch

This New Zealand jewel is a steal at $35 million. Nestled in Hauraki Gulf, Pakatoa is occupied by an "inactive" resort featuring 24 cabins, 38 cottages, a golf course and a restaurant. It's accessible from Auckland by boat or aircraft — and boasts its own runway so you won't have to parachute into your backyard.

Dive into Pakatoa Island by visiting *www.vladi-private-islands.de*.

Cerralvo Island's Size Can't Be Beat

If you're searching for lots of space to stretch your dollar, you can't beat the 35,000 acres offered by Cerralvo Island. With a list price of $35 million, that's unmatched seclusion for only $1,000 per acre. (Hold on while we check our math again ... Yeah, that's right.) Located off the east coast of Baja in the Sea of Cortez, the rugged island is undeveloped — perfect for the HGTV addict who craves a really challenging reno project.

Visit *www.lapaz-realestate.com* to size up Cerralvo Island.

Temptation Island Is Tempting

Hey, didn't they make a Reality TV program here? The 20-acre Temptation Island is located off the east coast of Phuket, Thailand, and features enough palm trees and white sand to melt the frost off the most frigid marriage. You won't have this romantic retreat to yourselves, though; a 132-guest resort was built on the island in 1989. Not sure if you think 132's a crowd, but for $30 million we'd expect more seclusion.

Get a reality check on Temptation Island at *www.private islandsonline.com.*

A Kingdom Lot Fit for a King and Queen

Looking to invest in a different kind of green? Why not fork out a few million for a few thousand acres of prime forestland? It's all the rage in New Hampshire and Maine, where affluent buyers are snapping up huge tracts of land. John Malone, head of Liberty Media Corp., has 53,000 acres in western Maine. Dick Brown, former head of technology services colossus EDS Corp., owns 20,000 acres not far from Malone's spread. Be prepared for some backlash from environmentalists and foresters (there are some odd bedfellows for you), who are decrying the loss of prime habitats and forestry jobs.

....

TipBit: Kingdom Came and Went

While not technically a kingdom lot, E. Stanley Kroenke's 145,000-acre Douglas Lake Ranch in British Columbia is certainly quite a spread. Kroenke, owner of the NHL's

Colorado Avalanche, bought the ranch from former MCI WorldCom chief exec Bernard Ebbers for $68.5 million. Ebbers, however, didn't see a penny; MCI's bankruptcy trustees pocketed all the proceeds.

Other Must-Haves to Make Your Home Magnificent

In this day and age, it's not enough to erect a multi-million-dollar mansion on an immense plot of land, throw up a 15-foot electric fence to keep out the Jehovah's Witnesses and call it home. What truly makes a house a home is the stuff you stuff inside it; those knickknacks and personal accents that bring the marble and alabaster to life.

Guided by the SKI-ing philosophy, we've highlighted some essential items that will boost your pad's warmth — and the rate at which you liquidate your bank account.

Do Not Strip this Wallpaper

The French company Zuber has been churning out the most expensive wallpaper in the world since 1797. The company handprints its panoramic panels from woodblocks, some of which of are older than Charlton Heston. Zuber's most expensive wallpaper is a panorama called *Les Guerres D'Independence* (The Wars of Independence), which consists of 32 panels and provides 49.4 feet of coverage. It sells for $40,500. Installation, but of course, is extra.

For more information, cut and paste *www.zuber.fr* into your web browser.

An Artful Strategy for Beautifying Your Home

Word has gotten out that well-chosen art can be a wise investment. "Art is now a distinct asset class and a diversification strategy, even for the ordinary buyer," says Elizabeth von Habsburg, president of New York City art consultancy Masterson Gurr Johns. See? Told you so.

How much should you be prepared to drop for a canvas? Plenty, because you'll face stiff bidding competition from *nouveau riche* American, Chinese, Russian and Japanese art fanciers. If it's a Picasso you're after, you'd best go high or go home. The first- and second-most-expensive paintings ever sold at action were both painted by the Cubist master. On May 4, 2004, his *Garcon à la Pipe* sold for $104.2 million, with commissions, besting the more recent sale of his *Dora Maar au Chat* on May 4, 2006. It went for a song: $95.6 million, including commissions. Just make sure you don't hang your new canvas over the Zuber wallpaper.

A Throne Fit for a King and Queen

The high-tech Neorest toilet made by Japanese company Toto, the world's largest toilet maker (there's a claim to fame), will flush between $5,000 and $5,200 from your bank account. Popular in modern Tokyo office buildings for years, the "hands-free" Neorest is still relatively unknown to most Westerners (who'll likely take a while to warm to this "hands-free" business). The hefty price stems from its slew of luxury features: front- and back-aerated warm-water spray (um, front *and* back?), oscillating spray massage, heated seat, catalytic air deodorizer and warm air dryer. The environmental benefits of the Neorest are more than enough to offset any guilt over the pampering; the toilet uses only 1.2 gallons of water per flush.

Visit *www.totoneorest.com* for the straight poop on the Neorest toilet.

bathtub for the master bathroom? Worth $1.1 million, six of the tubs have been purchased by the Mikazuki group of hotels for its chain. And you know the old saying: If it's good enough for Mikazuki, it's good enough for you!

Project Your Wealth with a Runco MBX-1

Make your home *the* home to watch C-SPAN reruns. Technically considered a television, the MBX-1 by Union City, California-based Runco is actually a mini-theater. Priced to move at a cool quarter million, you get a three-chip digital system with enough horsepower to project on screens as large as 41 feet wide. The real trick is finding 41 feet of wall space — and a seat far enough away to avoid a neck craning, front-row-of-the-theatre experience.

Visit *www.runco.com* to get the big picture on the MBX-1.

High Fidelity at a Sky-High Price

Your stacks of wax will never sound as good as they will on Rockport Technology's Sirius III turntable. The only system to garner a "Class A+" rating from *Stereophile* magazine (created specifically for the Sirius III, literally placing the turntable in a class by itself), the hardware takes 60 vendors six months to custom build and costs an astounding $90,000.

All this time, effort and money goes into producing a turntable with one purpose: Rotate the record album at an exact and constant speed.

You'd think that'd be child's play, right? Far from it. To achieve this lofty goal, the Sirius III uses 550 pounds of high-tech components that bear no resemblance to the J. C. Penney turntable that adorned your childhood basement. See if any of this hardware looks familiar: an active pneumatic isolation system (think anti-skip technology); a 185-pound epoxy-composite plinth; a 62-pound air-bearing platter machined from stainless steel bar stock; an air-driven spindle/motor-drive unit; an electronic motor-controller unit; an air-bearing tone arm system; and a compressor.

If you mistook the above for a home contractor's grocery list, you're forgiven. But these components, flying in tight formation, can yield speed accuracy in the order of 10 parts per million, according to Rockport. Nothing but hot air, you say? Actually, it's compressed air.

The Sirius III has no belts, springs, ball bearings or bushings to create vibrations or otherwise interfere with the graceful tracking of the tone arm across the record. The system's prime mover is compressed air. In fact, the only mechanical contact in the entire system is that between the stylus and the record. That's it on the freakin' list.

Those rare few who have experienced the Sirius III firsthand speak in reverent, quasi-orgasmic tones of its unparalleled performance. They also tend to be single men in their late 30s who build model airplanes when they're not scouring Internet chat rooms for original presses of the James Gang's pre-Joe Walsh albums, but we digress.

Finally, your Jan Hammer and Mott the Hoople discs will sound as crisp, clean and drug-addled as they did when you were a teenager.

Visit *www.rockport.com* today for a tune up.

TipBit: U.S. Estate Tax — Part II

In 2006, the U.S. Senate failed to approve a permanent repeal of the U.S. estate tax, despite (or due to?) strong support from the White House and many heavyweight Republicans. Democrats who opposed the repeal said it would have given trillions of dollars away to America's richest families. They also pointed out that, with the current tax exemption on an estate's first $2,000,000, fewer than one-fourth of 1% of estates in the U.S. would have been subject to the "death tax" in 2006.

Ferrari Unica Personal Gym

You passed up a Ferrari Testarossa in favor of buying the first U.S. model of the Bugatti Veyron and doing brake stands on your neighbor's lawn, so why not add a Ferrari universal gym to your stable? Nicely appointed with beige *Poltrona Frau* leather and Ferrari *Rossa Corsa* paint scheme, it even has an on-board computer to accelerate your fitness program. Drive it off the lot for $17,500.

Floor it to *www.ferrari-world.com* for details.

Robby, the Robot

Robby is seven feet tall, a bit on the chunky side for weighing only 100 pounds and retails for $49,999.95. A little steep, you say? Who cares! He's a freakin' robot.

Not just any robot, mind you. This animatronic, remote-controlled robot is manufactured by Fred Barton Productions and is identical to the one featured in the film *Forbidden Planet*. So, what does 50 large buy in a robot nowadays? Well, Robby can recite his lines from the film, as well as rotate his head and his many scanners. And at seven feet tall and 100 pounds, we're betting he can collect dust with the best of 'em.

Visit *www.the-robotman.com* for a huge, hulking piece of Hollywood memorabilia.

Closing the Door on Homes

O.K., that's just a peek at the architecture of the possible. A little taste to pique your appetite for the SKI-ing philosophy. But there's much more to life than life in your home. When you're not holed up inside your house, admiring the electric-blue glow of the Jehovah's Witnesses who tried to scale your perimeter fence warming the night sky, you're out and about, in motion. In Chapter 3, we'll explore how you can really get your motor running using the high-octane fuel of your kids' inheritance money.

Publisher's Note: *No Jehovah's Witnesses were harmed during the writing of this chapter. Nor does The FingerTip Press reserve special contempt for this religious group. Our contempt for all religious groups, sales people, telemarketers, family members and close friends who insist on "popping in" and otherwise invading our privacy is meted out in equal measure.*

*Wealth often takes away chances from men as well as poverty.
There is none to tell the rich to go on striving, for a rich man makes
the law that hallows and hollows his own life.*
— Sean O'Casey
"Pennsylvanian Visit," Vol. 5, *Rose and Crown*
Irish dramatist (1884–1964)

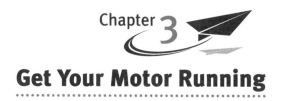

Chapter 3

Get Your Motor Running

People are tested by wealth, just as gold is tested by fire.
— Chinese proverb

The open road, open water and open skies hold a powerful allure for North Americans. The machines we use to carve the asphalt, H_2O and air perfectly embody the qualities we cherish in life: freedom, independence, autonomy and making the next-door neighbors wickedly jealous.

Our machines also represent an important linkage to our children. Remember the quality time spent with the kids in the A/C-free Ford Pinto, shuttling them over hell's half-acre in 100% humidity? How about those weekends at the cottage, skimming over the lake in the Bayliner Runabout, one hand on the steering wheel and the other on Junior's shirt collar as he yacked his last three meals over the side? Or the first time you took little Missy up in the Cessna Aerobat, only to unveil her acute aviophobia? Ah, memories are made of these.

By embracing the SKI-ing philosophy, however, you can create a new bank of memories that are mercifully devoid of cascading sweat, projectile vomit and eardrum-perforating screams. All it takes is a little imagination — and your entire life's savings.

TipBit: We Like to Move It, Move It

Americans love their vehicles. Collectively, they've registered billions of dollars worth of machinery. Consider these numbers from the U.S. Bureau of Transit Statistics while you consider your finances:

- ❖ 136,430,651 registered passenger vehicles in 2004
- ❖ 5,780,870 registered motorcycles in 2004
- ❖ 12,781,476 registered recreational boats in 2004
- ❖ 209,708 registered general-aviation aircraft in 2003

A Passion for Passenger Vehicles

In your pre-SKI-ing days, hitting the road in your car likely meant hopping into the minivan to run the kids to baseball practice, ballet or — during the more taxing teenaged years — parole hearings. Your second vehicle, assuming you were forward-thinking enough to stash some cash away before the kids were born, was likely a 10-speed Schwinn … or the shoes strapped to your feet.

As functional as these family vehicles were, they lacked a certain *je ne sais quoi* in the fun and cool departments. Especially the Schwinn. (Bike helmets and those ankle clips that prevent your Gap khakis from being eaten by the chain are decidedly unfun and uncool, no matter how you spin it.) By embracing the SKI-ing philosophy, however, you can kick down the doors to the fun and cool departments and enter with aplomb.

Now, when you think about the world's most expensive cars, you probably think Ferrari, Lamborghini, Rolls-Royce and Kia, right? O.K., maybe not Kia. But would it surprise you to know that *none* of these classics were featured in the *Forbes* Top 10 list for 2006? We hope so, or else we'll have a tough time getting you to read the next few pages.

The Top-Ten Kick-Butt Cars of 2006

No. 1: Bugatti Veyron 16.4

Who says the French are just cheese eating surrender monkeys? They certainly took no prisoners when they designed the Veyron 16.4. Plagued by production delays (it's France, the Mecca of production delays, after all), the most exclusive sports car ever built is finally ready to tear both road and driver a new one with performance only a jet fighter can beat.

The Veyron builds on Bugatti's sterling reputation for building untouchable race cars in the '20s and '30s. The company's production workshop, where no more than 70 vehicles per year will be hand built, is located in Molsheim-Dorlsheim, the same French town where Ettore Bugatti first set up shop nearly 100 years ago.

But enough history, already. Let's check out the most exclusive sports car's capabilities:

❖ The Veyron's W16 alloy engine delivers 1,001 horsepower, allowing the car to accelerate from zero to 60 miles per hour in three seconds flat … and beyond 200 miles per hour in a mere 14 seconds.

❖ The Veyron's top speed is a bladder-slackening 252.3 miles per hour. And it's the car's chassis and drive train that limit its top end, not the engine.

❖ The car's direct-shift gearbox allows the seven-speed gearbox to transmit power to all four wheels without interruption. For the mechanically disinclined out there, that translates into pure acceleration from zero to 252.3 miles per hour. Good luck finding anything comparable outside of the U.S. Air Force.

❖ The Veyron's rear spoiler, besides providing crucial down force at high speeds, acts like a drag parachute during extreme braking. With this baby's speed, that could come in *real* handy.

Sticker Shock: $1,192,057 (undercoating extra)

No. 2: PAGANI Zonda Roadster F C12S 7.3 (Clubsport version)

Besides *La Cosa Nostra* and enough backstory material for six seasons of the *Sopranos,* Italy has given the world many a fine sports car. Their latest gift is the Zonda Roadster. This 650-horsepower super-car sports a Mercedes-Benz engine and gives buyers the option of personalizing the interior. Have a rare leather in mind for the seats? PAGANI can deliver!

Sticker Shock: $667,321

No. 3: SSC Ultimate Aero

USA! USA! The most expensive American car in 2006 was also the fastest. SSC hasn't verified the Aero's top speed, but the manufacturer is confident the beast will hit between 260 and 273 miles per hour. It's set to challenge for the world top-speed record in Wolfsburg, Germany in May 2007. The car's modified, supercharged Corvette engine looks like it's up to the task; it

produces a testicle-tingling 1,180 horsepower. That'll get you from home to the nearest Starbucks in less time than it takes to place your order with the barista.

Sticker Shock: $654,500

....
TipBit: Millions of Millionaires

Speaking of the U.S., did you know the country is home to more millionaires than any other country? There are more than 2.7 million of 'em, hidden among the rest of us destitutes. If you stop to think about it, that means about one in every 100 people you flip off while driving has seven figures socked away under a mattress.

Here's how the numbers break down for other countries:

- ❖ United Kingdom: 448,000 millionaires
- ❖ China: 320,000 millionaires
- ❖ Canada: 230,000 millionaires
- ❖ India: 83,000 millionaires

And the source of wealth behind these numbers?

- ❖ 37% from business ownership
- ❖ 24% from income
- ❖ 18% from inheritance
....

No. 4: LeBlanc Mirabeau

This is the car you'd expect IKEA's Ingvar Kamprad to be driving — if he wasn't such a spendthrift and pushing, like, 90 years old. Switzerland's super-car is built to FIA/Le Mans standards, meaning it's a street-legal race car. (But not yet street-legal in the U.S.; the company has to do some tweaking before it receives the designation.) The Mirabeau has a Koenigsegg V8 under the hood, the same engine that drives the Koenigsegg CCR (see No. 6 on the list).

Sticker Shock: $645,084

No. 5: Saleen S7 Twin Turbo

What was the world's most expensive car in 2005 squeaks in at only No. 5 in 2006. Make no mistake, though; the Twin Turbo's recognition factor more than makes up for its diminished ranking. Incorporating the latest in modern racing technology, the Twin Turbo also brings a heaping helping of comfort to the table. A/C, power windows, remote keyless entry for the doors and both trunks (it's a mid-engine model), leather-strapped steering wheel and an AM/FM/CD/DVD/TV system all come standard (although using the word "standard" in connection with this car seems ignoble). Oh, and the Twin Turbo also comes with a video "rearview mirror" — a small video camera mounted in the rear of the car. Perfect for gauging how far the cops are lagging behind.

Sticker Shock: $555,000

The Rest of the Best

No.	Make & Model	Made In	Sticker Shock
6.	Koenigsegg CCR	Sweden	$540,000
7.	Mercedes-Benz SLR McLaren	Germany	$540,000
8.	Porsche Carrera GT	Germany	$440,000
9.	Mercedes-Benz Maybach 62	Germany	$400,000
10.	Mercedes-Benz Maybach 57S	Germany	$367,000

....
TipBit: Gunning for Grey Goose

Sidney Frank, creator of Grey Goose vodka, recently bought a $400,000 Mercedes-Benz Maybach and then dropped another $100,000 to make it bullet proof. Frank reportedly flies the car back and forth between his homes in New York and San Diego.

Frankly, for that price we'd be driving the car for all it's worth. Then again, Frank may have a good reason for not driving it too often. Probably the same reason that led to bulletproofing the car in the first place.
....

Awesome Automobiles at Auction

If buying off the lot and losing 10% of the car's value the moment you turn the key in the ignition isn't for you, why not get your dream wheels at a classic-car auction? The Barrett-Jackson Collector Car auction in Scottsdale, Arizona draws hundreds of thousands of collectors (and millions more via TV) every year, generating hundreds of millions in sales. In 2006, the most expensive vehicle auctioned off was a 1950 General Motors Futurliner Parade of Progress tour bus, which fetched over $4 million after auction fees.

Sticking with the auction theme, the RM Auctions sale in January 2006 featured the James Bond Aston Martin DB5 and a 1928 Cadillac Town Sedan customized for Chicago mobster Al Capone.

The DB5 came complete with concealed machine guns, rear bullet-proof shield, rotating license plates, tire shredders, an oil-slick dispenser, a car phone and a tracking device. The passenger-side ejection seat, unfortunately, was removed before the auction.

Capone's Caddy featured the same black-on-green paint scheme used by the Chicago Police Department in the 1920s (so rival gangs would be caught with their pants down when his hit-men drove up). Rumor has it the very car on the auction block was used in the Valentine's Day massacre. The car's unusual options include a chop-down rear window (handy for firing Tommy guns at pursuing vehicles: "You'll never take me alive, copper! *Muyah,* see, *muyah*") inch-thick, bulletproof glass and a police siren.

RM Auctions sold the Bond DB5 for $2,090,000, while Capone's Cadillac was a steal at $621,500.

TipBit: U.S. Estate Tax — Why Can't We Let This Go?

Stop the presses, there's more to this story! Two weeks after efforts to repeal the U.S. estate tax failed, as reported in **U.S. Estate Tax — Part II,** lawmakers voted to exempt the first $5,000,000 of an estate's value from taxation for individuals (or $10,000,000 for couples!), and to index the limit to inflation. Well, Zip-a-Dee-Doo-Dah. Raise your hand if this even remotely affects your life. C'mon, raise it high. Yeah, we didn't think so.

Mad for Motorcycles

Cue the Steppenwolf soundtrack and break out the leather chaps for something other than "Get-Your-Freak-On" Fridays. It's time to go hog wild! We're not talking off-the-rack bikes, guys and gals. We're talking original, his-and-hers custom builds.

Today's choppers are chrome-plated, exquisitely airbrushed works of art. Look no farther than the Discovery Channel's *American Chopper* for an example of the detail that goes into these steel horses. Expect to drop anywhere from $75,000 to $200,000 or higher, especially for the one-of-a-kind bikes you see on television. Make sure you save a few bucks for lessons, though; dropping one of these babies because you forgot to lower the kickstand will earn you a well-deserved, year-long sentence as a weekend Chuck E. Cheese employee. And you're getting off lightly.

But you can't put a price on the kind of *Cool* these machines bring to the table. Those bugs in your teeth never tasted so good!

Bonkers for Boats

Ah, life on the ocean waves. Heaven for millions of North Americans; hell for the millions who suffer from chronic seasickness. Oh well, sucks to be them. For those who feel a nautical calling, however, the SKI-ing philosophy allows them to set sail in more than a 12-foot aluminum skiff. Here's a sample of the seafaring style SKI-ing affords.

Playing Yacht-Sea

Fancy yourself a man of the sea, but have nothing to test your sea legs on? How about hitching a ride aboard *Le Grand Bleu,* the 370-foot private yacht owned by Russian oil billionaire Roman Abramovich? Built for an estimated $135 million in Vulkan, Germany in 2000, it comes with a 72-foot sailboat, a 59-foot motor cruiser, a helicopter and — get this — a submarine. It's listed as the world's fifth-largest private yacht by *Power and Motoryacht* magazine. Former owners include Microsoft's Paul Allen and Seattle businessman John McCaw.

....

TipBit: Size Does Matter

Many yacht aficionados speculate Oracle CEO Larry Ellison ordered a last-minute increase to the length of *Rising Sun,* his 450-foot luxury yacht, in order to outdistance Paul Allen's 414-foot *Octopus* and earn the title of the world's largest yacht owner (um, let's make that *owner of* the world's largest yacht ... Larry's waistline is pretty slim). Technically speaking, however, two yachts beat *Rising Sun* to the finish line: the 456-foot *Al Salamah,* owned by the Crown Prince Sultan of Saudi

Arabia, and the nearly 525-foot *Platinum/Golden Star* owned by the Sheik of Dubai.

Technically speaking (again), however, the folks who keep track of this trivia exclude yachts owned by heads of state. So, technically speaking (yet again), Ellison's *Rising Sun* is the largest privately owned yacht in the world.

Good grief, who else needs a bottle of rum?

Own the Ocean Waves

Millennium Super Yachts is asking $28 million for its 137-foot *The World is Not Enough*, billed as the world's fastest yacht. Crewed by eight and appointed for 10 passengers, *The World* features walnut bulkheads (walls to you landlubbers), marble and alabaster heads (bathrooms), two Jacuzzis and a smattering of 42-inch plasma TVs.

If speed is of the essence, this is the yacht for you. Capable of making 70 knots (80 miles per hour), it'll outrun most major warships and coast guard vessels (if that's important to you) and more than halve the travel time between exotic ports over other yachts. And the less time the crew spends driving the bus, the more time they have to cater to your every whim.

TipBit: Sardinia's Super-Fees for Super-Yachts

While you're cruising the Mediterranean in your super-yacht, you might want to skip Sardinia's exotic ports of call. In 2006, the island's regional government introduced a luxury tax that applies to second homes, yachts and private aircraft in order to capitalize on the steady stream of billionaires who enjoy hitting the Emerald Coast every

summer. Any yacht longer than 30 meters (roughly 100 feet) will have to pay a berthing fee of nearly $30,000 or more, a rate 50 times higher than nearby destinations like Corsica.

Buy a Land Boat

So, you tried the sea-faring shtick and wound up more nauseated than the audience at a Céline Dion concert, huh? Maybe you need a Recreational Vehicle. Now, we know what you're thinking: Randy Quaid in *Christmas Vacation*, right? Guzzling a beer in his bathrobe while he pumps liquid waste from his RV into a storm sewer. Get that image out of your mind and replace it with a 36-foot palace on wheels, complete with Jacuzzi, plasma TV, marble countertops, more floor space than your first apartment and a custom paint job that makes Bon Jovi's tour bus look like a graffiti-tagged Westphalia minivan. And don't worry if you're not a graying retiree; the average RV buyer today is 35 to 55 years old. So, go on, drop a quarter million and pimp that land boat.

TipBit: How Do You Spell "Plutonomy?"

Take the plutocracy, the governing elite of society, and stitch them onto the economy. Besides an excuse to grab a dictionary, what do you get? The "plutonomy." This new term, coined by analysts at Citigroup, describes the impact of the *crème de la crème* of the wealthiest people on the economies of the U.S. and Canada. Actually, Citigroup's head of global equity strategy, Ajay Kapur, has identified the U.S., Canada and Britain as countries whose economic growth is powered by — and largely consumed by — a wealthy few.

Besides hiring analysts at Citigroup to coin obscure terms to describe their activity, on what do these "plutonomic" groups unload their coin? Oh, the usual stuff: private equity investments, hedge funds, art and upmarket properties. On the latter, central London seems to be one of the hottest markets for swish properties — and many buyers are paying cash for cribs worth up to $30 million.

Ardent for Private Aircraft

Air travel today is as close to the Bataan Death March as you can get without being taken prisoner by a fanatical Japanese officer who's been holed up on a remote Pacific island since World War II. (Private island buyers beware!)

There's the requirement to arrive at the airport obnoxiously early. (What's the rule now? Show up, naked, six hours prior to your flight?) Shakedowns by security personnel you wouldn't trust to light your barbecue in order to remove nail clippers, hair gel, shampoo and shaving cream from your carry-on baggage — and every vestige of dignity from your psyche. And all this to endure a leg-cramping, gastric nightmare, squeezed into a 12-inch-wide seat between a guy who hasn't showered since Reagan was in office and a woman whose nervousness has short-circuited her mouth's "off" switch?

It's no wonder well-heeled North Americans are turning to ownership as a remedy for the terminal decline of air travel. Owning your own aircraft jets you to the head of the line at the airport. And the time saved when you're carting kids who start asking "Are we there yet?" before they finish packing is worth its weight in frequent-flyer miles. Then there's the ability to pick and choose your destinations — and fly to them directly. As anyone who's endured a multi-city milk run can attest, the perk of flying a straight line between here and there is priceless.

When it comes to acquiring your own private jet, you have a number of options. And just like when you're shopping around for a pack of smokes after a half-dozen wobbly pops at the bar, your choices when it comes to getting jets fall into the light, medium and heavy categories.

Light, medium and heavy, of course, refer to the size of the jet, not the passengers. Size makes a big difference when it comes to number of people you can cram on board and how far you can fling them. Here's a handy table for your comparison-shopping pleasure:

	Light	**Medium**	**Heavy**
Aircraft	Citation Bravo	Hawker 850XP	Global Express
Passengers	7 (max)	8 (max)	19 (max)
Max Speed	373 knots	419 knots	562 knots
Max Range	1,400 nm	2,598 nm	6,700 nm
Price	$4 million (used)	$13.6 million (new)	$40 million (used)

Each of the preceding jets comes complete with plush cabin interiors, featuring pedestal-mounted swivel chairs, ample leg room and a wet bar to take the edge off the latest Orange Alert. The Global Express, not surprisingly, offers the most versatility with respect to cabin configuration. It can easily transform into an airborne office, stateroom, conference center or strip club on the fly. It's also the only aircraft on the list that can jet between any two points on earth with only one pit stop for refueling. Luckily for you and your passengers, the cabin is fitted with washrooms, 'cause that's a long stretch between gas stations.

If you like the convenience offered by aircraft ownership, but are less enthralled by the expense, don't worry. Time sharing and fractional ownership allows you to buy a piece of the action. Jet Networks' time-sharing business model features Gold, Platinum and Black memberships for a $100K, $250K and $500K deposit, respectively. Members then pay an hourly fee for their travels, ranging from $3,200 to $7,400 depending on the type of jet used.

NetJets uses a fractional-ownership business model, where you actually purchase a percentage interest in a particular aircraft. The lowest fractional share available is one-sixteenth of a Hawker 400XP, and that'll set you back $406,000. NetJets, by the way, is a wholly owned subsidiary of Warren Buffett's Berkshire Hathaway.

....

TipBit: Choose Sentient Jet for a Rapid Departure

Sentient Jet of Weymouth, Massachusetts spawned the private-jet-membership business model in 1999. It offers Silver or Gold memberships for deposits of $100,000 or $250,000 a pop, and you can book flights on a fleet of 900 participating aircraft and have the hourly cost debited from your membership account.

Like Jet Networks and NetJets, Sentient's choice of aircraft falls into the Light, Medium (Mid-Sized) and Heavy categories. Hourly rates for preferred jets range

from $3,300 to $9,800 for travel within the continental U.S., $3,300 to $10,780 for travel to Mexico and the Caribbean and $4,800 to $13,400 for intra-Europe travel. The company reports that demand for private jets to the Turks and Caicos in the Caribbean has soared 80% in the past year.

Best of all, membership with Sentient allows you to book flights with only 10 hours' notice. Ideal for staying one step ahead of the kids — or the law.

Shifting Gears

All right, that should be more than enough inspiration to spark your imagination and your spending engine. Now, let's shift into overdrive and accelerate like a Bugatti Veyron toward some exciting destinations that lay beyond your own backyard. It's a big planet, and it's beckoning you to come out and play.

Next stop, luxury travel.

Let no man get by inheritance, or by will, more than will produce at four per cent interest an income ... of fifteen thousand dollars per year, or an estate of five hundred thousand dollars.
— Rutherford Birchard Hayes, *Diary and Letters of Rutherford Birchard Hayes: Nineteenth President of the United States,* vol. IV
U.S. president (1822–1893)

Wealth I ask not, hope nor love,
Nor a friend to know me;
All I ask: the heaven above
And the road below me.
— Robert Louis Stevenson
British writer, essayist, poet & novelist (1850–1894)

Chapter 4

Have Cash, Will Travel

Upon the standard to which the wise and honest will now repair it is written: "You have lived the easy way; henceforth, you will live the hard way ... You came into a great heritage made by the insight and the sweat and the blood of inspired and devoted and courageous men; thoughtlessly and in utmost self-indulgence you have all but squandered this inheritance..."
— Walter Lippmann
American essayist & editor (1889–1974)

The travel bug afflicts millions of North Americans. A grand total of 61,776,000 Americans visited 23 top-ranked foreign destinations in 2004, according to the latest figures from the Office of Travel and Tourism Industries. Canadians fled their snow-packed country in droves in 2005; 19,983,000 of them mushed dogsleds to 15 primo countries. That's a combined total of over 80 million people scouring tourist shops for the picture-perfect postcard.

Now, in your pre-SKI-ing days your summer travel plans might have been limited to weekend forays to Aunt Maude's, where you and the kids would endure her psoriasis flare-ups and Crisco-drenched cooking. For the more adventurous, there might have been a week-long odyssey at DisneyWorld/Land, where you shared the dubious magic of Mickey's kingdom with 5.7 million sugar-infused children and their ready-to-dive-head-first-off-Cinderella's-Castle's-ramparts parents. Perhaps, if you dislike crowds and money-siphoning amusements, there were longer summer trips to take in North America's resplendent national parks. Nothing says "vacation" like sharing the wonders of nature with 5.7 million black flies — unless you throw in the added chance of being eaten alive by grizzlies (after you've been eaten alive by the black flies, of course).

Maybe there was foreign intrigue involved in your travels with the kids. It's hard to match the intrigue involved in locating children's aspirin to cut your daughter's fever in a country where the only phrase you know how to say is "I am becoming a toilet. Please help me know when I can see it."

TipBit: Foreign Destinations are the Tops

Curious to know where most North Americans travel when they travel abroad?

Here's a rundown to help you avoid them:

Top Five Foreign Destinations for American Travelers in 2005

- ❖ Mexico: 20,325,000 American visitors
- ❖ Canada: 14,390,000 American visitors
- ❖ United Kingdom: 3,829,000 American visitors
- ❖ France: 2,217,000 American visitors
- ❖ Italy: 2,044,000 American visitors

**Top Five Foreign Destinations for
Canadian Travelers in 2005**

❖ United States: 14,862,000 Canadian visitors
❖ United Kingdom: 898,000 Canadian visitors
❖ Mexico: 794,000 Canadian visitors
❖ France: 616,000 Canadian visitors
❖ Cuba: 518,000 Canadian visitors

Wow, talk about your similarities. Though we can't figure out why Cuba didn't make the U.S. Top Five list.

The most galling part of family vacations — besides not recognizing the most galling part of family vacations 'til years after the fact — is that the kids don't even remember 'em. Seriously. Ask any 25 year old where she went vacationing with her parents when she was a kid and all you'll get is a blank stare, followed by "I had parents back then?" Take your children anywhere before they turn 13 years old and you might as well be taking a cardboard cutout.

It's an ironic truth of life that by the time the kids are old enough to remember family vacations, they would rather walk naked through their high school cafeteria during lunch hour than be seen anywhere with Mom and Dad (a.k.a. "the Geezers"). But imagine the kind of trips you can take once you free yourself from the need to save for your kids' inheritance — and from the need to take the kids with you. Forget stamp collecting in your golden years; embrace SKI-ing now and start collecting one-of-a-kind experiences. And forget roughing it, too. Luxe travel is back, baby!

After a long hiatus following the tragedy of September 11, 2001 luxury tour operators are again reporting record sales of opulent escapes. Like never before, affluent Baby Boomers — and a significant number of well-heeled younger couples — are

opting for the best luxury travel has to offer. Around-the-world private jet charters. Exotic cruises that take you off the well-trodden track. Safaris in Botswana. Anything other than camping at Jellystone during black-fly season.

TipBit: The Ultra-Rich are Rootless

There was a time when the über-rich would buy a huge estate in the countryside, put up a 15-foot electric fence and settle into a sedentary life of counting gold coins in the family-room vault while quacking like Scrooge McDuck.

Today's wealthy, however, pull up more tent pegs than carnies – and stay one step ahead of the tax man in the process. They might have a winter hang out in Ibiza, an apartment in New York and homes in three different time zones. Nearly every globetrotter, however, has a place to flop in Britain; non-domiciled residents who were born outside the country pay no tax on income earned overseas, so long as they spend fewer than 183 days in Britain and follow certain rules regarding property ownership. Rumor has it that nearly one-third of Monaco's population speaks with a British accent and is appalling in bed. Consult your lawyer for details!

There's Diamonds in Them Thar Hills!

Back in 1991, two prospectors named Charles Fipke and Stewart Blusson triggered Canada's biggest staking rush when they discovered diamonds at Point Lake in the Northwest Territories. And just like the gold rush of last century, it wasn't long before some enterprising companies stepped forward to mine silver from the pockets of adventurers with a taste for cool, crisp ice. Horizon & Co., a Canadian travel company, has come up with a great idea — and it'll only set you back $160,000. Billed as a once-in-a-lifetime trip, Horizon's Winter Ice package jets you and your *amour* to exotic Yellowknife, dogsleds you to a private wilderness camp replete with a well-appointed post-and-beam lodge and lets you hand pick a rough diamond from the factory floor. You'll watch as the stone is cut and polished to perfection for your beloved — and as your beloved withers under the unyielding romantic pressure. Then, just when you think the romance index can't climb any higher, they'll laser engrave your message of love into the precious gem.

This trip has all the teethmarks of classic movie romance: breathless adventure, the magnificent desolation of the frozen north, sparkling diamonds and the musty funk of damp husky fur. Let's face it; if you don't get lucky on this trip, *you never will.*

Mush your way to *www.horizon-co.com* for more information.

Nine Wonders a Wonder to Behold

Abercrombie & Kent, the luxury tour operator, has put together a private-jet vacation package that blows the doors off any packaged vacation you've ever experienced. Over the course of 23 days of pampered travel, you and your betrothed will fly to nine wondrous areas of the world aboard a private 757 jet outfitted for 48 paying passengers.

The landmarks of world culture and history selected for this journey include:

Flores, Guatemala: Home to El Petén, which features Central America's largest tropical rainforest and Tikal National Park. In

Tikal, you'll take in scads of ruins from the ancient Mayan civilization. A & K have thought of everything, so you're safe to leave your umbrellas at home.

Easter Island, Chile: You and your fellow passengers will likely outnumber the indigenous population of Easter Island, one of the most isolated places on the planet. Located 2,347 miles off the coast of Chile, the island features immense ceremonial statues known as *moai*. Come to think of it, didn't Godzilla and his fellow monsters hang out here? Oh, right, that was *Christmas* Island. (Pesky nuclear testing!) Anyhow, be sure you don't miss the plane while you're here; paddling 2,347 miles back to Chile in a dug-out canoe could really put a cramp in your style — and your rowing arm.

Sydney, Australia: Thoroughly modern Sydney harbors ancient Aboriginal culture and more exotic wildlife than you can shake a

wombat at. For the daring, climb atop the catwalks of Sydney Harbour Bridge and spit on the traffic passing below.

Siem Reap, Cambodia: Here in Siem Reap, you'll see the ruined cities of Angkor, a complex of temples, palaces and terraces built between the ninth and fifteenth centuries A.D. The perfect place to buy and flip some property? We think so!

Yangon, Myanmar: Hop back onto the jet after low-balling some Cambodian real-estate developers and hop over to Yangon, where you'll visit the dazzling Shwedagon Pagoda. This incredible structure is gilded with more than *eight tons* of gold, so be sure to bring a cutting torch. Like they're going to miss a pound or two? And if they do, you can be sure your adventure tour of Myanmar's penal system will prove even more memorable than the Nine Wonders.

Jodhpur, India: Assuming you make it out of Myanmar with the rest of your fellow passengers, the next stop is Jodhpur in northern India. The city's ancient walls surround a hodge-podge of narrow streets and colorful bazaars. Now would be a good time to start wearing the money belt.

Agra, India: You can't visit India without visiting the Taj Mahal, and you won't thanks to A & K's peerless planning skills. This 350-year-old mausoleum is a monument to undying love, erected by Emperor Shah Jahan in memory of his wife Mumtaz Mahal. And to think you have trouble remembering your anniversary.

Dubai, United Arab Emirates: After being browbeaten by your wife on the marble steps of the Taj Mahal for your lame demonstrations of affection, you'll head off to Dubai, where you can hopefully lose the little missus in the city's warren of gold and spice souks — or in the Wild Wadi Water Park.

Petra, Jordan: The ruins-of-the-ancient-world tour continues in Petra, home to the famous "Lost City" of Petra. Take a horseback ride to the *Siq* — the contorted cleft of rock that served Petra's ancient builders as a natural fortification against invaders. Guess it worked, considering the whole damned city was lost for hundreds of years.

Cairo, Egypt: Jet to Cairo for the last stop of this magnificent tour. Meet Dr. Zahi Hamass, Secretary General of the Supreme Council of Antiquities (and avid eBay trader, we wager) who'll regale you with his insights into the Pyramids and Sphinx. Then, just when you're sick to death of hearing insights into the Pyramids and Sphinx, journey to see them first hand. You'll also get an insider's glimpse of the newly discovered Workmen's Tomb, which hasn't yet opened to the general (read: raggedy-assed) public. Cool! That means the Pharaoh's Curse will be nice and fresh.

O.K., who else counted 10 wonders? Let's see, there's Flores, Easter Island, Sydney ... yep, that's 10 alright. Either A & K can't count, or we plugged a destination they don't consider to be a wonder. Oh, well. Whether it's nine or 10 wonders of world culture and history, the price is still $69,875 per person. How wonderful is that?

Wondering if this trip is for you? Find out at *www.abercrombie kent.com.*

....

TipBit: SKI Club Australia

SKI Club Australia is a tongue-in-cheek, family-owned and operated website based in, you guessed it, Australia. It aims to be a one-stop, online shop providing products and services tailored specifically for Baby Boomers with a healthy sense of humor and a burning desire to poach their nest eggs. According to creators Michelle and Bob Lamont, the site will also function as an international forum for those who want to exchange ideas, information and SKI-ing stories.

Michelle Lamont says the website concept rose "phoenix-like" out of a comment made by an elderly couple to her then 57-year-old husband at a famous (and expensive) resort town in southeast Queensland. The elderly couple noted how they were happily spending their kids' inheritance — with the encouragement of their kids. Husband Bob recognized a golden opportunity, and SKI-ed with it.

SKI your way to *www.skiclubaustralia.com.au* and get inspired.

Roughing It Ain't So Rough Anymore

Thanks to the Four Seasons Tented Camp in Chiang Rai, Thailand, you may have to rethink your aversion to roughing it. Accessible only by riverboat, the Four Seasons' camp features 15 tented accommodations with hand-hammered copper bathtubs, air conditioning, high-speed Internet access and hardwood flooring. Optional activities while you're there include learning to drive an elephant mahout style (we'll leave that to your imagination), exploring the Mekong River via customized riverboat, formal campfire dinners (without a s'more in sight) and riverside drinks in a stilt-top bar. At $1,675 per room per night, you may never leave …

Luxury Cruises: Not Your Mother's *Love Boat*

Anyone who's witnessed a buffet-table cattle drive or attempted to steal a quiet moment among 1,500 passengers knows this: cruise ships can leave plenty to be desired. Today, luxury means much, much less ... people, that is. And for those seeking the best high-seas cruising has to offer, luxury means a return to sail and men at masts that always lean.

Floating on a *Sea Cloud*

Built for financier E. F. Hutton ("When E. F. Hutton speaks, people shut the %#$@ up") in 1931, the 360-foot *Sea Cloud* was — at the time — the largest private yacht in the world. The four-masted barque (a type of Tall Ship) was designed for a singular purpose: to convey Hutton and his wife, Marjorie Merriweather Post, to whatever destinations their business and pleasure took them, in the level of comfort to which they'd become accustomed. Oddly, the yacht was also employed as America's Russian embassy in the late '30s, after the land-borne embassy was found to be bugged. The yacht's two owner cabins and eight deluxe cabins were designed and furnished by Merriweather Post, who spent two years poring over designs to achieve her exacting vision of luxury. Here's a description of Owner's Cabin No. 1, once occupied by Lady Marjorie herself:

❖ *Cabin Size:* 410 square feet.

❖ *Furnishings:* Portholes, a generous sitting area, Louis XIV-style bed and nightstands, table, decorative marble fireplace, desk, walk-in closet and a safe for your diamond jewelry.

❖ *Bed:* King-size bed with two separate mattresses.

❖ *Bath:* 97 square feet with tub, water closet, bidet, marble sink, golden swan fixtures, dressing table, hairdryer and outlet for razor. Bath completely outfitted in white Carrara marble, with two additional portholes.

That's quite a cabin. And with room for only 64 passengers, *Sea Cloud* is the ideal vessel for plying the Mediterranean and Caribbean. Seven days from $4,800 to $17,200 per person.

Sail by *www.seacloud.com* for more information.

TipBit: Thrillionaires

JPMorgan Asset Management recently hired a cultural anthropologist to research what makes wealthy people tick. The conclusion? The wealthy fall into one of five categories, three of which are witty enough to share with you below:

❖ *Thrillionaires:* Those most likely to blow their money on acquiring fabulous objects and experiences.

❖ *Willionaires:* Those who feel a responsibility to leave the world a better place. Voted most likely to donate a library wing or have a music hall named after them.

❖ *Realionaires:* Those people who are loaded, but drive a crappier car than yours.

Abercrombie & Kent Small Ship Cruising

Experience a trip rated by Condé Nast as the best cruise of its type in the world. Ply the waters of Antarctica aboard the 198-passenger *Explorer II*. Get up close and personal with seal-dotted icebergs aboard *Explorer II*'s smaller exploratory vessels. Guest

quarters include terraces, satellite TVs, bathtubs and epic views of whales and penguins. Enjoy sumptuous cuisine before gathering for an evening natural history lecture by onboard experts. Or get loaded on fine wine and skip the lecture if you had more than your fill of natural-history lectures in college. Minimum 10 nights from $6,650 to $18,750 per person.

Explore the possibilities at *www.abercrombiekent.com.*

The World

What's like a cruise ship, but isn't a cruise ship? It's *The World*, a 644-foot, 12-deck luxury ship built in Norway. Owned by residenSea, *The World* perpetually plies the oceans to deliver its wealthy passengers — residents, actually — to all the fabulous ports their fabulous bank accounts can afford.

The World's residents drop an average of $2,100 per square foot for a luxe suite, putting the average digs in the $2.3 to $7.5 million bracket. Those without a net worth of $5 million need not apply.

Besides smashing pads, *The World* boasts four restaurants, a handful of bars, a cigar bar, library, art gallery, Internet café … everything a decent city offers, except panhandlers. And with residents limited to 600 people, you won't have to wait long to check your e-mails or light your stogie.

Visit *www.residensea.com* for more info.

The *Annaliesse*

If you want to take the 279-foot *Annaliesse* out for a week, be prepared to pay top dollar. Known as the most expensive private yacht charter in the world, the *Annaliesse* is owned by entrepreneur

Andreas Liveras. The ship comfortably holds 36 passengers, and has a one-to-one guest-to-staff ratio. Her sun deck rises an incredible 71 feet above the water's surface, and her main saloon is straight out of the pages of the *Robb Report;* teak furniture; silk curtains; Michelangelo marble columns; a 51-inch TV; ideal for viewing *White Squall* on a storm-tossed night; and a grand piano that really gets the boat a' rockin'. The *Annaliesse*'s master suite features 1,313 square feet of living space, with 180-degree panoramic windows and a private deck. A California king-size bed and twin Jacuzzi mean you'll never have to set foot outside the cabin.

You can opt for custom-designed cruises of the Caribbean, Mediterranean and Sicily for as little as $847,000 per week. And if you're in the market for this kind of unmatched luxury, you can cough up $95.5 million. The yacht, you see, has been on the selling block since January 2006.

Visit *www.AndreasLiveras.com* and make him an offer he can't refuse.

....

TipBit: Out of Space in Africa

Classic Africa, the Middle Haddam, Connecticut company operating safari tours that run over $60,000 per person, recently had to turn down requests for high-end safaris because there are too few spots available.

....

Welcome to Hotel Can't Afford Ya

Odds are better than average you'll need a place to flop while you're traveling the world, if only to have somewhere to store the souvenirs. Thanks to the SKI-ing philosophy, your choices extend beyond the foreign equivalent of a Salvation

Army Men's Mission. In fact, the best hotel suites the world has to offer bear no resemblance to the dingy rooms you usually relieve of towels and mini-soaps. Don't believe us? Take a look.

Has Anyone Seen The Bridge Suite?

Here's a riddle for you: What has 826 acres, accommodates over 1,200 guests and had a starring role in the Pierce Brosnan and Woody Harrelson film, *After the Sunset*?

No, it's not Kirstie Alley. It's the Atlantis, a luxury resort on Paradise Island in the Bahamas. It boasts the Bridge Suite, home to the priciest night of slumber you'll ever stumble upon in your travels.

Nicknamed the Disneyland for the rich and fabulous, the Atlantis opened in 1998 at a cost of $475 million, and is now the largest family resort of its type in the world. No wonder. It features 35 restaurants, bars and lounges, as well as designer shops and 11 swimming areas with water slides that drop from Mayan-style temples. If you're wondering how the resort got its name, find out when you stroll through a "faithfully re-created" ancient Atlantis (where'd they find the blueprints?) and end up staring into one of the world's largest aquariums.

As luxurious as the resort is, the opulence really kicks into high gear inside the Bridge Suite. Nestled between two enormous, pink seahorses 16 stories above the sand, the 10-room suite is saturated in gold and glass. Panoramic, floor-to-ceiling windows provide unobstructed ocean views, and the personal chef and butler provide unobstructed molly-coddling. And all it costs for one night in the suite is a decent down payment on an average home: $25,000.

The Emirates Palace isn't for Profit

The paint is hardly dry on the doors of the Emirates Palace, the most expensive hotel ever constructed. Rumored to have cost over $3 billion to build, it's owned by the government of Abu Dhabi and will likely never see a profit.

Profit, however, was never the goal with the Emirates Palace. Impressing the living hell out of guests and the world at large was, and on that score the designers succeeded in spades. The hotel's entrance arch soars vertically to 131 feet and traverses 118 feet from side to side. That makes it just a tad smaller than the Arc de Triomphe in Paris. The lobby's atrium dome is larger than that of St. Paul's Cathedral, and is topped by a six-foot finial made of solid gold. The hotel has 16 Palace Suites, where lucky travelers will be treated to:

❖ Personalized registration in the privacy of the suite.

❖ 61-inch plasma screen in every bedroom, living room and dining room.

❖ Flower arrangement in the suite.

❖ Complimentary bath preparation and evening turn-down service.

❖ 24-hour butler service.

❖ Complimentary beverages and snacks in the suite throughout the day.

Hey, if you eat your own body weight in M&Ms and macadamia nuts, the $15,000-per-night fee works out to be pretty reasonable.

Come Sail Away at the Burj Al Arab

Fancy a game of tennis at 690 feet above ground level? How about a few nights at what's been described as the world's boldest hotel? Fulfil both dreams at the Burj Al Arab in Dubai.

Designed to resemble a billowing sail, the Burj Al Arab is built on a manmade island and, at 1,053 feet high, is billed as the world's tallest building used exclusively as a hotel. You won't find anything like this along the I-95. Its *smallest* suite has over 1,800 square feet of floor space, while the largest suite occupies nearly 8,400 square feet and will set you back over $15,000 per night. And the high-altitude tennis? That's the height of the hotel's helipad, where Andre Agassi and Roger Federer played an unranked match in February 2005 to promote the Dubai Duty Free Men's Open.

Visit *www.burj-al-arab.com* to get served more info.

....

TipBit: The Most Expensive
Night's Sleep in America

Outside of spending the night with your mistress — and getting caught — the most expensive night's sleep in the U.S. is found in the Presidential Suite at the Plaza Hotel in New York. Occupying the lion's share of the hotel's eighteenth floor, the 7,802-square-foot suite features five bedrooms, five-and-a-half bathrooms, two living rooms, a dining room and a sauna. Toss in several fireplaces, a wine cellar and a killer view of Central Park, and it's easy to understand why the Plaza wants — and gets — $15,000 per night.

Sojourn to the west coast and you'll find the second-most-expensive hotel room at the Fairmont in San Francisco. At 6,000 square feet, the Fairmont's Penthouse Suite has the usual amenities you'd expect to find in a

hotel room: a dining room fit for 50 dinner guests, a two-story library, a billiards room decked out in floor-to-ceiling Persian tile and bathrooms fitted with 24-karat-gold fixtures. For an insider's peek at the Penthouse Suite, rent *The Rock*. It's where Sean Connery gets his haircut (and dangles a cop off the eighth-floor balcony). A night in the Penthouse will cost you $10,000 — extra if you want to shear Connery's locks.

You won't have to travel far to find the third-most-expensive hotel room. Besides an impressive décor — the description of which we'll spare you here — one of the grace notes that makes the Penthouse Suite at the Regent Beverly Wilshire worth $7,500 per night is the hotel's pre-stay interview to discover your every whim and fancy. Want a gross of Vienna sausage, a barrel of pickled cabbage and six wheels of Limburger waiting for you when you open the penthouse door? Simply specify in advance. But don't expect to stay again if that's the direction your taste leans.

The Bellagio Villas at the Bellagio in Las Vegas settle in at fourth place. Each of the nine villas has a private terrace and pool, private butler service and a private limousine entrance for camera-shy high rollers. Two-bedroom villas will run you $5,000 per night, while the three-bedrooms go for $6,000. That still leaves plenty of cash to lose at the craps tables.

The last stop on the list is the Mansion at the MGM Grand, a mere stone's throw from the Bellagio. Here, you'll find private accommodations in a 2,900-square-foot villa for $5,000 a night, and have access to two private chefs 24/7, just in case you're hankering for Kraft Dinner after a long night of playing the slots. Say "Hi" to Gil Grissom for us!

Get Away From It All

For truly discerning travelers, it isn't enough to get away from it all. They really want to *get away from it all*. If you count yourself among this rarified group, here are three ultimate escapes without comparison.

Buy a Piece of the World Islands

Just down the shore from the Burj Al Arab, you'll find a collection of islands shaped like the continents of the world. Once completed in 2008, the World Islands will consist of 300 artificial islands that are divided into four categories: private homes, estate homes, dream resorts and community islands.

The size of each island will range from 250,000 to 900,000 square feet, with 164 to 328 feet of water between each to act as a privacy buffer. At 5.4 miles in length and 3.6 miles in width, the area covered by the entire development will total nearly 19.5 square miles and be contained within an oval breakwater.

Individual islands will be sold off to private developers, and are expected to fetch $6.85 million and up. Given a total construction cost of $1.8 billion, the consortium behind the World Islands stands to make a pretty penny.

If you want to own a piece of the World Islands, however, you'd better move fast. Sir Richard Branson has already snapped up "Great Britain."

A Trip That's Out of This World

Speaking of Sir Richard Branson, have you heard about his latest business vehicle, Virgin Galactic? It happens to be a rocket ship, and the company expects to begin launching paying customers into orbit by late 2008 or early 2009.

Building on the success of SpaceShipOne, the innovative spacecraft that won the $10 million Ansari-X Prize in October 2004 as the first private spacecraft to fly into space twice in a two-week period, Virgin Galactic has contracted with Burt Rutan's Scaled Composites — the company that designed and built SpaceShipOne — to build five spacecrafts capable of carrying passengers 60 miles into the air for $200,000 apiece. Virgin Galactic also recently announced a deal to build a $225 million spaceport in New Mexico, near the White Sands Missile Range.

TipBit: Put Your Money into Orbit

Here's yet another example of why your money is better spent on something other than your kids. The financial muscle that made Burt Rutan's spacecraft design fly came from none other than Microsoft co-founder, Paul Allen. Allen's Mojave Aerospace Ventures was the sole financial backer for SpaceShipOne. Think your kids will create a legacy as great as viable commercial space travel with their inheritance money?

Yeah, we didn't think so, either.

So, what kind of experience will $200,000 buy you? Unlike the Apollo astronauts, you won't experience a bone-jarring blast-off from ground level. The Virgin Galactic spacecraft will be hoisted to an altitude of 10 miles by a larger aircraft, or mother ship, much like the sound-barrier-busting X-1 rocket piloted by Chuck Yeager. This launch configuration gets you into the "thin air" without using tons of heavy — and volatile — rocket fuel.

At the appointed altitude, the latches release and you separate from mother. Your spacecraft drops a few dozen feet before its rocket ignites, then mounting g-forces squeeze you into the seat as you accelerate to three-and-a-half times the speed of sound — faster than a bullet from a gun. The flat horizon changes to an azure-blue curve as you climb higher and higher. Above, the sky darkens. Stars appear, even as the sunlight grows stronger and sharper.

At 60 miles above the earth, the rocket engine cuts off, plunging you into silence so stark you hear every beat of your pounding heart. Gravity's tug slows your ascent until, for the most fleeting of moments, you pause at the very apex of the climb. Then, it's all downhill. In this phase of the flight, you feel none of gravity's effects. You're free-falling back to earth, weightless. At 50,000 feet, Rutan's unique design turns the spacecraft into a glider and you touch down on the runway at the New Mexico spaceport.

Just imagine how good your next meal will taste after this adventure. But worth the $200,000?

Every damn penny.

TipBit: The Russians are a Blast

For 100 times the price of Virgin Galactic's adventure, you can hitch a ride on a Russian Soyuz rocket. The Russian Space Agency insists you undergo an extensive six-month training regimen at the Gagarin Cosmonauts Training Center in Star City, however, before you blast off. (Pesky Russian bureaucracy!)

U.S. businessman Dennis Tito became the world's first space tourist when he launched as part of the three-person Soyuz TM-31/32 mission to supply the International Space Station in April 2001. For a ticket price of $20 million, he received seven days in low-earth orbit, including two days in the International Space Station (under the watchful eye of the American astronauts onboard). Rumor has it that Tito was not permitted to enter the American segments of the space station unescorted. Guess NASA was worried he might open the wrong hatch.

A Trip That's *Really* Out of this World

The only certain things in life are death and taxes ... or are they? A select group of North America's wealthiest are determined to prove the saying wrong. They're taking advantage of a tax loophole to bequeath their wealth to themselves. Their dead selves, not to put too fine a point on it.

No, they're not delusional. They're applying good ol' North American ingenuity to changes in the length of time money can be held in trust. Until recently, you see, trusts could only be established for a maximum of 21 years. Some wealthy individuals, however, found the timeline to be inadequate; a poor financial decision or unforeseen economic circumstances could impoverish future generations. Money placed in trust for a longer period could escape such setbacks, leaving a nest egg for the great-great-grandkids.

An unexpected offshoot of the longer time period is the rise of so-called "revival trusts." The money placed in these trusts isn't set aside for the great-great-grandkids; it's earmarked for the revived version of your corpse.

"But wait a second," you say. "Won't my corpse be kind of, you know, gross a long, long time from now?"

Not if you take the appropriate steps to preserve it. By freezing their bodies and using personal revival trusts, wealthy individuals can sock away millions of dollars until future technology makes it possible to reanimate their dead selves. The individuals name their frozen corpses as beneficiaries (and, no, "frozen corpses" does not mean their wives), which — for legal purposes — treats them as unborn grandchildren.

If your deep freezer isn't deep enough to accommodate your bulk, don't worry. The Alcor Life Suspension Foundation of

Scottsdale, Arizona has you covered. For fees ranging from $80,000 to $150,000, Alcor will cryogenically preserve your brain and/or entire body. Basically, there are four steps involved:

❖ *Select Your Option:* Will that be head and brain only, or your entire body?

❖ *Arrange Payment:* That'll be $80,000 for the head and brain, $150,000 for the entire body. Tip is optional, but add $25,000 for international surcharge if you live outside the U.S. (Canadian surcharge is only $10,000.) If you're short on cash, you can set up a revival trust using a life-insurance policy that names Alcor as a full or partial beneficiary. Remember to keep a little something for yourself, though. Who knows how much a pint of milk and loaf of bread will cost in 2350?

❖ *Die:* Preferably in Scottsdale, Arizona. If you lack the foresight to die near the Alcor facility, the next best option is to expire when medical practitioners are close at hand. *Very* close at hand. You see, certain procedures, if carried out immediately after death, greatly increase the odds of a successful revival. The brain and body deteriorate quickly once the blood stops pumping, so the administration of anti-clotting agents, cardiopulmonary support to achieve maximum circulation of the anti-clotting agents and rapid cooling are vital. Kick off in your apartment and go undiscovered for a month and all bets are off.

❖ *Check In:* For a really, really long time. Your stay at Alcor begins with perfusion, a process that replaces your blood with an organ-preservation solution, ideal for supporting life at extremely low temperatures. Once thoroughly perfused, you'll be slipped into a sleeping bag and chilled to –196° Celsius (the temperature of liquid nitrogen) over a period of 200 hours. Once chilled, you'll be transferred to a large vat for long-term storage. Amenities include a 10-foot-tall, stainless steel container, thousands of gallons of liquid nitrogen and absolute peace and quiet. You might even share your "living" space with baseball great Ted Williams, who's been on ice at the Alcor facility since 2002.

Not convinced this option is for you? Well, call it (frozen) food for thought.

THAT'S IT! IF THEY DON'T TURN UP THE HEAT IN THIS ROOM, WE'RE GOING TO ANOTHER HOTEL!

....

TipBit: Timing to Die

The Australian government abolished its federal inheritance tax at the stroke of midnight on July 1, 1979. More recently, two Australian economists dug into the country's death records, just for sh*ts and giggles, and made a startling discovery. Compared to other years, there were noticeably fewer deaths in the last week of June 1979 — when the deceased would have been taxed up to 28% of their estate's value — and the first week of July 1979, when they could expire tax free. How's that for brilliant tax planning?

....

Bring It On Home

If you embrace the SKI-ing philosophy, your passport will soon be filled with colorful stamps from exotic locales, your mind with one-of-a-kind memories that will last a lifetime, and your bank account with many hefty withdrawals.

We hope you'll squirrel away a little something for the items highlighted in the next chapter, however. Now that you've pimped your home, your vehicles and your travels, it's time to pimp yourself ...

Um, that's probably not the best way to put it. Just read on and you'll figure out what we mean.

Wealth is an inborn attitude of mind, like poverty.
The pauper who has made his pile may flaunt his spoils,
but cannot wear them plausibly.
— Jean Cocteau
French author & filmmaker (1889–1963)

The loss of wealth is loss of dirt,
As sages in all times assert;
The happy man's without a shirt.
— John Heywood
English dramatist (1497?–1580?)

Chapter 5

Gadgets and Baubles and Bling, Oh My!

To dic rich is to die disgraced.
— Andrew Carnegie

ere we go, into the home stretch! Raise your hand if you're not yet convinced of the SKI-ing philosophy's benefits for both you and your kids. O.K., a few of you are still on the fence, despite a taste of the lip-smacking opportunities SKI-ing offers for your home, your vehicles and your travels. (Not to mention the benefits it affords your kids!) Not to worry; this chapter will provide the final helping that'll send your taste buds spinning head-over-heels in love with unbridled SKI-ing.

If you're like most parents, you've given up plenty to give your children round-the-clock lifestyle support. Hours of precious sleep. Every drop of spare time. Your dreams of becoming the next Dale Earnhardt and/or Lucy Lawless.

But one of the most common things parents abandon while raising Junior and Missy to be law-abiding citizens are the items that fall into the "nice-to-have" category. You know, *prezzies;* those personal gifts that have little impact on day-to-day living, but a major impact on how much we enjoy day-to-day living. Imagine, however, how it would feel to give yourself incredible gadgets and baubles and bling, making your eyes light up like they used to on your birthday — presents stretched before you like an endless summer day — when you were a kid.

Ouch! Sorry for that last metaphor. But the final benefit of spending your kids' inheritance should not be underestimated. Putting that magical sparkle back in your eye is possible if you turn *every* day into your birthday. And you can when you're SKI-ing.

Many happy returns.

....

TipBit: Up to the Hilton with Paris

When it comes to billionaire heiresses, there's but one blazing light on the American landscape. Paris Hilton, great-granddaughter of Hilton Hotels founder Conrad Hilton, garners more ink on a weekly basis than that expended on Stephen King's entire body of work. Ever expanding her repertoire, Paris recently ventured into the music industry, where the public's taste flits from artist to artist like fruit flies at a farmer's market. Will the public's taste for Paris' vocal renditions have a longer life span?

We can't summon the energy to care.

Burning with less intensity, but just as brightly, is Julia Louis-Dreyfus. Louis-Dreyfus seared her name into the nation's consciousness as Elaine Benes on *Seinfeld*, and has kept the flame alive with her work in *The New Adventures of Old Christine*. She's earned millions thanks to her comedic talent and well-honed acting chops, but did you know she's also a billionaire heiress? Her father is French billionaire Gérard Louis-Dreyfus, chairman of the

Louis-Dreyfus Group, whose interests include real estate, agricultural products, petroleum and other commodities. He was ranked No. 200 on the 2006 *Forbes* list, with a net worth of $3.4 billion.

Also forging a shining path for other billionaire heiresses to follow is Dylan Lauren, daughter of fashion designer Ralph Lauren. She's turned a sweet tooth into sweet profits with Dylan's Candy Bar stores in New York, Long Island, Houston and Orlando. Hey, someone has to catch the South Beach dieters when they fall. Dylan's Candy Bar has also developed its own clothing line, Candy Couture. Inedible, unfortunately.

Spider-Man Dress

Got an extra $9.5 million to spare? That's what Scott Henshall's mind-blowing Spider-Man dress will set you back. Made up of approximately 3,000 diamonds and fashioned into an intricate spider's web, the dress is unique, to say the least. It's also used, however. Samantha Mumba wore it to the premiere of *Spider Man II* in September 2004. Yeah, that's what we thought: Samantha who? Here's a more important question, though. What on earth do you wear for accessories when you're wearing a diamond dress?

A Fantasy Bra to Dream About

Running with the diamonds-and-designs theme, how about a Victoria's Secret Fantasy Bra to wear beneath the Spider-Man dress? The 2006 model features 2,000 Hearts-on-Fire diamonds and a flawless 10-carat cleavage brooch (that's flawless diamond, not flawless cleavage … though a 10-carat rock tends to detract

from any flaws in that department, but we digress). The bra is worth $6.5 million, nearly half the price of last year's Sexy Splendour bra. Perhaps Victoria's Secret is hoping to actually sell one of its annual Fantasy Bras?

Go bust by visiting *www.victoriassecret.com.*

··

TipBit: Ice, Ice, Baby!

Did you know there are only about 300 major diamonds in the world? The *crème de la crème* is the De Beers Millennium Star Diamond, plucked from a mine in the early 1990s by workers whose daily wages couldn't buy a decent latté in Minneapolis. (Wait a second, can *anyone* buy a decent latté in Minneapolis?)

The Millennium Star Diamond is flawless, both inside and out, and weighs in at 203 carats. Diamond experts haven't been able to price the pear-shaped stone because they lose the ability to think in its presence.

··

Let Your Boots Do the Talkin'

Shoes are a woman's signature item. Or obsession, depending on your viewpoint. Maybe that's why American women dropped nearly $17 billion on fashionable footwear between October 2004 and October 2005, according to the NPD Group. But rather than scrawl your mark with an "X," the SKI-ing philosophy enables you to indelibly stamp your name in gilt-edged loafers.

The highest-priced heels into which you can squeeze your twinkly toes are attached to a $14,000 pair of alligator boots from Manolo Blahnik. Next up is a pair of Vienna Minimalisa High Boots from Louis Vuitton. These stylish, ostrich-leather beauties will cost you $4,500. If pumps really rev you up, Chanel's $2,875 alligator-and-lambskin numbers will get your heart a' pumping.

And what goes better with a gorgeous pair of shoes than a smashing new purse? The only one that can hold its own against your five-figure Manolos is Fendi's "B.Bag." It hangs out in the five-figure territory, too: $25,000.

Tie One On

Let's face it, guys. If your lady's wearing the Spider-Man dress, Manolo boots and carrying a B.Bag, you'll have to step up your fashion game. Out with the Limp Bizkit hoodie, in with a signature tie. Here's one you'll be sure to keep out of the soup bowl. It was created by Satya Paul for the Suashish Diamond group. Handcrafted from pure silk, the tie is adorned with 150 grams of white gold and 261 diamonds (77 carats' worth). It's said to be worth one crore. One crore, as everyone knows, is 10 million rupees or roughly a quarter million U.S. dollars. Really, guys, keep it out of the soup bowl.

This'll Suit You

The broad-shouldered, hip-hugging suits fashioned by Brioni ooze authority — and hair gel if you forget to put the lid back on the tube in your front pocket and then sit down. Don't worry; you won't do it twice. The favorite of such style moguls as U.N. Secretary General Kofi Annan and Brand Secretary General Donald Trump, a nattily tailored Brioni suit will run you up to $7,500 in whatever material your material heart desires.

Suit up at the Brioni boutiques in New York and Beverly Hills, or visit *www.brioni.it.*

Grilling Time for a Perfect Ass

How about a new set of choppers to replace that picket fence inside your mouth? For $50,000 you can get dental implants that'll make Ryan Seacrest's grill look like a barbecue pit. Always making a perfect ass out of yourself in public? Well, now you can pick up the perfect posterior with a set of buttock implants. A steal at $5,000 per cheek.

This Pen is Costlier than the Sword

With the glut of high-tech communications technology at our fingertips, you'd think the lowly pen would be going the way of the dodo or Stephen Baldwin's acting career. For those with a fetish for ink on paper, however, Montblanc's *Bohème Royal* fountain pen keeps the writing off the wall for the humble writing stick.

The *Bohème Royal* Black & White is a made-to-order work of unparalleled precision and beauty. It calls for master craftsmanship on the part of the seller — and an incredible looseness with money on the part of the buyer.

A jewel setter requires six months to cut 56 facets into each of the pen's 1,430 black and white diamonds. He then delicately places the stones side by side, creating a perfectly smooth, pave-set surface for your dainty fingers. The jewel setter then, no doubt, grabs his high-powered rifle and heads for the nearest clock tower to relieve the gnawing tedium. Then, he returns to the shop to set the half-carat diamond that sits atop the pen's lid.

Buyers should take note that using a Montblanc pen requires a modicum of skill. Too much pressure on the nib or an improper angle between the nib and paper can cause leakage. Mind you, with all those diamonds you're sure to attract the right kind of attention while you mangle Sudoku puzzles at your local coffee shop.

Price tag? $150,000.

Write to *www.montblanc.com* for more info on the *Boheme Royal*.

Catalog Shopping for the Über-Wealthy

Looking for great holiday gifts? Look no further than the annual Neiman Marcus *Christmas Book*. The 2006 edition featured a 2007 BMW Limited Edition M6 Convertible and a behind-the-scenes tour of BMW's Munich plant for $139,000. Catering to the discerning shopper with an eye for the eclectic and a blockbuster bank account, the catalog's past gifts have included a $50,000 designer tree-house built from indigenous wood selected only from fallen trees, a $125,000 Maserati Quattroporte and a private 90-minute concert by Sir Elton John for $1.5 million. We have to wonder, though, whether Sir Elton can still fit into a Christmas stocking.

....

TipBit: Memmo to Self — Hire Hit Man to Kill Dad

A 34-year-old Shillington, Pennsylvania man was arrested in February 2006 on charges he tried to hire a hit man to kill his father. Jason Memmo was busted after offering an undercover state trooper $7,500 to off Memmo's dad, whose continued existence above ground was interfering with the younger Memmo's plan to inherit $250,000.

....

The Sweet Smell of Excess

Want to cause a real stink with the kids over their dwindling trust fund? Drop by Harrods of London and buy a bottle of Imperial Majesty, made by the *Roja Dove Haute Parfumerie*. A 500-ml bottle of the pricey perfume will cost you over $215,000. It comes with a five-carat diamond and an 18-karat-gold collar, so you might want to wear the bottle as a dynamite accessory at your next gala dinner. Remember, just a little dab'll do ya (and cost ya, like, $10,000).

And Tom Cruise Isn't Even Tending the Bar

After you've dropped over 200 large on a 500-ml bottle of perfume at Harrods, you'll probably need a good, stiff drink. Sashay over to the Sheraton Park Tower Hotel's Piano Bar in Knightsbridge for a Louis XIII cocktail.

Made with a liberal dose of Remy Martin Louis XIII, the finest cognac in the world, the drink comes with a sugar cube, two drops of Angostura bitters, Charles Heidsieck champagne and an armed guard. The concoction is lovingly poured into a crystal martini glass and finished off with ice. Ice as in diamonds, that is. A one-carat chaser, to be exact.

How much for this ice with a slice? $7,500.

....
TipBit: Now That's the Oyster's Ice-Skates

A perfectly formed pearl, everyone knows, starts with a grain of sand and ends after a whole heap of irritation. Want a perfect way to irritate your kids? Buy yourself a strand of South Sea pearls — the queen of all gems — for $300,000. Trust us; when the kids learn how much the necklace depleted their inheritance, they'll be plenty irritated.
....

A.A. for the Super Affluent

After a few weeks of downing Louis XIII cocktails, you'll need this next item. For $3,000 a day, you can hire your own sobriety coach. Rumor has it that Matthew Perry had one accompanying him to the set of *Friends* during the entire 2001 season.

If you've been on a particularly mind-bending bender, consider signing up for a one-month, individually tailored sobriety program at the Passages Rehab Clinic in Malibu for $39,550.

A Timely Way to Squander the Kids' Inheritance

Timex may take a lickin' and keep on tickin', but the company's affordable timepieces won't dish out much damage to your bank balance. For a real financial pasting, your watches gotta get glittery — and complicated.

For women's watches, it's the jewels that jack up the price. Take Chopard's "Super Ice Cube." Besides Swiss movement, the lucky lady wearing this watch gets over 60 carats' worth of diamonds: 1,897 brilliants, 288 trapeze cuts and a center case set with 16 squares. O.K., take a deep breath 'cause it's time for the price. Ready? How's $1,130,620 sound?

Rather than take the glittery route to stratospheric prices, men's watches grow more costly as they grow more complicated. (What is it with men and their love of complications?) Any watch constructed with four or more complications is known as a "grand complication."

What on earth is complication, you ask? Besides running into your wife when you're on a date with your mistress, a complication is any technical embellishment built into a watch, like a chronograph, lunar-phase indicator, perpetual calendar function, minute repeater or tourbillion (a nifty gadget that eradicates timekeeping errors that can arise due to tiny variations in gravitational effect as the watch moves).

So, which men's watch represents the biggest complication for your net worth? That'd be Blancpain's "1735," the timepiece named for the year Swiss watchmaker Jehan-Jacques Blancpain opened his first factory. The 1735 features six complications, a 42-mm platinum case and a crocodile strap. Best order one today, though; it'll take 10 months to assemble its 740 components. And 10 monthly payments of $100,000 each to strap it around your wrist.

If you have the time, visit *www.chapard.com* or *www.blancpain.ch* for more information.

TipBit: How Do You Spell Inheritance?

Aaron Spelling, whose gifts to the world of television included such classics as *Beverly Hills 90210*, died on June 23, 2006 and left behind an estate worth an estimated $300 million. His gift to his daughter, actor Tori Spelling, was apparently as thin as her acting talent, however.

The gossip mill was frothing like a Peach Pit milkshake over Tori's miniscule cut of Daddy's loot — less than $1 million in cash and stocks, according to "insiders." Tori blames a falling out with her mother, Candy, for the financial snub. Candy, naturally, denies the allegation.

A Monopoly on Games Night

You might want to reconsider purchasing a limited edition of Monopoly if you're the kind of player who scatters the board when you lose. The top-of-the-line version is bound in alligator skin and comes with customizable solid-gold playing pieces and gilt-edged money.

Originally marketed by Parker Brothers in the U.S., the exclusive edition is manufactured by Essex-based Geoffrey Parker, Ltd. in Britain. (No relation, just a quirky coincidence.) The luxe version retails for over $900,000. If that's a little steep for a board game that'll likely be stuffed inside a non-descript cupboard for months at a time, you can opt for a downscaled version with pewter playing pieces for $5,500. Even the poor man's version will have you thinking twice about tossing a tantrum — and the board — when you lose to your kids.

Tee Off the Children

Tired of getting blanked in the win column when it comes to games with the kids? Treat yourself to a good walk wasted on the links, and do it in solitary style with a set of Honma golf clubs. Manufactured in Japan to your exacting specifications for length and weight, you can also select the precise head shape, shaft size and the amount of 24-karat gold plating and platinum detailing. A set of 14 clubs will set you back about $50,000. Need we warn you not to chuck these clubs into the water hazard after you four-putt on the back nine?

Rubik's Masterpiece Cube

O.K., here's a game you're sure to throw away in disgust, despite its jaw-dropping $1.5 million price tag. Actually, "game" might be stretching it, as the term usually denotes "fun." There's nothing fun about the Rubik's Cube. This diabolical gadget has been around since the mid-'70s, driving mathematically challenged knuckle draggers around the bend with its 43 quintillion possible combinations.

In the mid-'90s, Diamond Cutters International created the Masterpiece Cube, a fully functional cube pimped out with 22.5 carats' worth of amethysts, 34 carats' worth of rubies and 34 carats' worth of emeralds, all mounted on an 18-karat-gold frame.

The world record for solving the cube, by the way, was set by some knob at the California Institute of Technology in January 2006. He did it in 11.13 seconds. We recommend hurling the Masterpiece Cube in his direction when the time comes. And aim for the head.

....

TipBit: The Grave Consequences of Inheritance

In 1999, an Argentinean inheritance battle over Rufino Otero's estate took a macabre turn when his grave was desecrated. Otero, a wealthy landowner, left $30 million to his widow when he died in 1983. All was well and fine until his widow passed away and passed the fortune on to Otero's nephew. In 1999, a previously unknown, illegitimate daughter appeared out of the wilderness to contest the inheritance.

A judge ordered the exhumation of Otero's body so a DNA sample could be obtained for comparison to the alleged daughter's DNA. The case entered Edgar Allan Poe territory when another body was found in the grave. After years of legal wrangling, another judge recently ordered the exhumation of Otero's parents for a last-gasp sample. Don't be surprised if you see the nephew at the local Home Depot, buying another shovel.

···

···

TipBit: A Diamond is Forever ... Unlike You
On the off chance you forego cryogenic preservation when you die, Rusty VanderBeisen has come up with a method for extracting carbon from the human body during cremation. Diamonds, you'll recall from high school chemistry (or not), are merely chunks of carbon that have been subjected to tremendous pressure over a long period of time. VanderBeisen's Life Gem Memorials will put the squeeze on your ashes and produce a one-carat stone for $22,000. That should be just enough to cover the cost of the wedding when your widow gets remarried.

···

The company of just and righteous men
is better than wealth and a rich estate.
— Euripides, *Ægeus,* Fragment 7
Greek tragic dramatist (480 or 485–406 B.C.)

The Last Word

Well, here we are. Safe and sound at the end of the digest. Bet the journey didn't hurt half as much as you imagined it would, did it? We'll also wager the glare from the emotional quotient of SKI-ing has faded. Maybe even enough to let the benefits of the philosophy come shining through.

If you received *Blow Your Bank Wad* as a gift from your kids, pat yourself on the back for raising upstanding children who aren't afraid to make their own mark in life. If you bought this digest with your own money and suddenly find it missing from the nightstand, however, watch out! Your kids might see its message as a threat to their planned life of leisure after you slip this mortal coil.

Assuming you found your original copy or bought a replacement and found a better hiding place, you can finally see how the SKI-ing philosophy liberates your mind from the crushing obligation to fund your children's future lifestyle. And, relieved of the pressure, you've probably noticed bright, new horizons appearing from the haze. Whether they relate to your home or your vehicles or your travels or your bling, they offer fresh, enticing destinations. Sure, they may seem impossibly remote right now, but be patient. Give your mind – and your bank account – time to absorb the power of the SKI-ing philosophy and the distance will start to shrink.

And as the distance shrinks, be sure to let us know about your tales of SKI-ing. Drop us a line at *tad@blowyourbankwad.com* or *alicia@blowyourbankwad.com* and tell us the wonderful ways you're poaching that nest egg.

And remember: it's never too late to start. All it takes is the decision to plunge into SKI-ing's warm, inviting waters.

Go on. Take the plunge today.

Cool Resources

Here are 20 handy titles to help reinforce the principles of the SKI-ing philosophy – or help you do some real estate planning (that's *real* estate planning, not real-estate planning) if you chicken out and decide to actually leaving something for the kids. *Bok-bok-bok.* Trust us. Once you go cross-eyed reading about wills, probate, living trusts and so on, you'll realize how much easier it will be to just spend everything instead!

50 Fabulous Places to Retire in America by Arthur Griffith and Mary Griffith, February 2006.

1,000 Places to See Before You Die: A Traveler's Life List by Patricia Schultz, May 2003.

Areal Diffusion and Genetic Inheritance: Problems in Comparative Linguistics (Explorations in Linguistic Typology) by Alexandra Y. Aikhenvald and R. M. W. Dixon, April 2006. Oops, wrong kind of inheritance!

AARP Crash Course in Estate Planning: The Essential Guide to Wills, Trusts, and Your Personal Legacy by Michael Palermo, December 2004.

Confessions of an Heiress: A Tongue-in-Chic Peek Behind the Pose by Paris Hilton, Merle Ginsberg and Jeff Vespa, September 2004.

Estate Planning for Dummies by Jordan Simon and Brian Caverly, March 2003.

Everything a Baby Boomer Should Know by Mark Cornwell, April 2006.

How Much Is Enough?: Everything You Need to Know to Steer Clear of Overindulgence and Raise Likeable, Responsible, and Respectful

Children by Jean Illsley Clarke, Connie Dawson, David Bredehoft, Ph.D. and David Walsh, December 2003.

How to Enjoy Your Retirement, Third Edition: Activities from A to Z by Tricia Wagner and Barbara Day, June 2006.

How to Love Your Retirement: Advice from Hundreds of Retirees by Hundreds Of Heads, Barbara Waxman and Bob Mendelson, August 2006.

How to Retire Happy, Wild, and Free: Retirement Wisdom That You Won't Get from Your Financial Advisor by Ernie J. Zelinski, March 2004.

How to Spend the Kids' Inheritance by Annie Hulley, August 2006.

Overcoming the Inheritance Taboo by Steven J. Hendlin, June 2004.

Plan Your Estate (8th Edition) by Denis Clifford and Cora Jordan, March 2006.

Prime Time: How Baby Boomers Will Revolutionize Retirement and Transform America by Marc Freedman, March 2002.

Raising Self-Reliant Children in a Self-Indulgent World: Seven Building Blocks for Developing Capable Young People by H. Stephen Glenn, Ph.D., and Jane Nelsen, Ed. D., June 2000.

Retire Secure! Pay Taxes Later: The Key to Making Your Money Last as Long as You Do by James Lange, August 2006.

The New Retirement: The Ultimate Guide to the Rest of Your Life by Jan Cullinane and Cathy Fitzgerald, July 2004.

Too Much of a Good Thing by Daniel Kindlon, January 2003.

Your Complete Retirement Planning Road Map: The Leave-Nothing-to-Chance, Worry-Free, All-Systems-Go Guide by Ed Slott, December 2006.

Index
....

About The FingerTip Press

A Simple Mission from a Simple Company
Run by Simple People

The FingerTip Press is proud to bring to you the *Tipping Points Digest* series — trade paperback originals, e-digests and audio digests tailor-made for time-crunched readers.

Tipping Points Digest books are written for the tired, huddled masses who are stretched to the breaking point by the competing demands of love and labor (the work, not child-bearing kind). We promise to pack our books with the freshest and funniest lifestyle and relationship tips and deliver them in the freshest and funniest formats, because nothing helps smooth over life's rough patches better than a spackle of humor. And if we make a little bit of money fulfilling our promise, we're o.k. with that, too.

But The FingerTip Press is more than just a money-grubbing publisher. (If you saw our income statements, you'd wholeheartedly agree!) We're devout believers that when it comes to our work lives and our love lives — and the stress each can impose on the other — nothing works better than humor to get us through the day. We've created two programs to help spread our gospel. We hope that after you've read about them you'll help spread the word as well!

The FingerTip Press'
At-Work Attitude Adjustment Program

Businesses throughout North America and around the world are letting huge profits slip through their fingers.

Employees throughout North America and around the world are feeling more overworked and stressed than ever.

It doesn't have to be this way!

The FingerTip Press' **At-Work Attitude Adjustment** program is designed to foster a more positive attitude toward our work lives. It seeks to promote awareness among management and employees alike on the many benefits humor can bring to the workplace. It aims to dispel the myth that work isn't supposed to be fun.

Hard work doesn't have to be *that* hard!

What the Program Is *Not*

The **At-Work Attitude Adjustment** program is *not* a fee-based, consultative program.

Some companies pay "humor doctors" huge sums for keynote speeches and full-day seminars. Frankly, we believe the task of boosting humor is best left to those working within your workplace, to company insiders who know the lay of the land and the governing politics. Our program provides simple tools and simple strategies your staff can implement with ease. **Simple works.**

The **At-Work Attitude Adjustment** program is *not* about prop comedy or Andrew Dice Clay stand-up routines. We're not trying to spawn a dozen Howie Mandel clones in your office (perish the thought) or turn your customer reception area into an R-rated night club. Like we said, the program's about simple tools and simple strategies. **Simple works.**

The **At-Work Attitude Adjustment** program is *not* some half-baked, airy-fairy concept dreamed up by liberal-arts majors. Well, not entirely.

While the publisher of The FingerTip Press does hold a Master's degree in Political Science, he has also experienced the value of humorous, stress-releasing activities first hand during his former career as a Naval Officer. If something as simple as humor can increase morale and cohesion in a warship patrolling for al-Qaeda suspects off the coast of Iran, you can bet your Argyle socks it'll help pull your marketing department together. **Simple works.**

So, what's the **At-Work Attitude Adjustment** program all about?

Simply put, it's a humor-advocacy program for fostering **positive attitudes** regarding our work lives. It seeks to **increase awareness** among management and employees alike on the urgent need to introduce more humor in the workplace — and humor's **many benefits.**

Remember the power — and profits — concealed beneath this simple equation:

More Humor = More Productivity = More Profitability

The FingerTip Press' At-Home Attitude Adjustment Program

Our **At-Home Attitude Adjustment Program** reaches out to *Tipping Points Digest*'s readers to promote the relationship benefits of shared reading at home, as well as the therapeutic benefits of laughter for enhancing intimacy and reducing relationship stress.

We like to call it **The FingerTip Fifteen.**

The FingerTip Fifteen:
A Prescription for What Ails Your Relationship

Driving. Working. Child rearing ...

Cooking. Bill paying. Sweeping ...

Vacuuming. Shaving. Sleeping ...

Ever notice how 99% of the day is spent doing serious stuff, or performing tasks so routine you could do them with your eyes closed?

Ever notice how 99% of the day is spent isolated from your partner — the very person you chose to spend the rest of your life with — even when you're both in the same room?

Ever wonder where the magic went? Ever wonder if you can get it back?

The FingerTip Press is here to give the magic back to you — along with a new attitude toward your relationship.

All we ask is that you give us 1% of your day ... just fifteen minutes of your time in order to reconnect with your partner. Fifteen minutes to laugh and bond — and maybe even get a little somethin' somethin'. Here's our simple prescription for curing what ails your relationship:

❖ Run, don't walk, to your favorite bookstore or specialty retailer that carries fine books. Check out *www.tipsdigest.com* for a list of *Tipping Points* dealers near you. (If you hate running, you can order directly from the site.)

❖ Seek out our *Tipping Points Digest* titles. Look for the biggest crowd, the mob where people are tearing each others' hair out to get near the shelves. That's for the latest *Harry Potter* or *The Da Vinci Code.* We're located in the self-help or humor section. Ask the nearest employee for directions.

❖ Purchase a *Tipping Points Digest.* Be pleasantly surprised that you can still afford to pick up milk and carb-conscious bread on the way home.

❖ Run, don't walk, home with your *Tipping Points Digest.* Don't forget to pick up milk and carb-conscious bread.

❖ Choose an appropriate time to read your *Tipping Points Digest* with your partner. If we might be so bold as to make a suggestion, the perfect time might be just before you go to sleep tonight.

❖ Take your *Tipping Points Digest* to bed and spend just fifteen minutes reading it aloud with your partner. Take turns. Make up funny voices. Share the illustrations. Laugh. Cuddle. Laugh some more. And maybe, just maybe, you'll spend another fifteen minutes doing something else before you fall asleep. O.K., maybe five minutes, then.

Upcoming Titles

Ho-Ho-Holy Crap!: More Than 101 Last-Minute,
Relationship-Saving Gift Ideas for Holiday Procrastinators

by Richard Steven Mack

How many times has the holiday season snuck up like a stealth bomber, forcing you to buy gifts for your better half in less time than it takes to soft boil an egg? If you're Richard Steven Mack, the answer is too many. He's learned the hard way that holiday-season procrastinators — both male and female — risk a bunker-busting bombshell in the form of an irate or hysterical partner if the prezzies don't measure up.

Watch for *Ho-Ho-Holy Crap!* at your favorite bookstore or specialty retailer ... and cross TV Guide and AA-batteries off your gift list forever.

* ❖ Active listening skills so you can tune into the hints your partner drops year round.

* ❖ The right time of day and week to hit the malls — and when to avoid them like your hot ex.

* ❖ The stores that can save your a** in an emergency.

* ❖ The gifts that seem perfect, but will land you in divorce court if you dare go there.

* ❖ The right and wrong ways to bribe your children to do your gift shopping.

Look for excerpts and sample chapters at *www.tipsdigest.com*

Visit *www.tipsdigest.com* Today!

www.tipsdigest.com is a refreshing watering hole for revitalizing your life. Think of our virtual space as your favorite pub — without the bar tabs, blackouts and raging hangovers. Like your favorite pub, *www.tipsdigest.com* is the best place to pick up the hottest ... um, tips, advice and life-enhancing strategies from people who have been there, done that, and worn the freakin' t-shirt down to its last threads.

Here are four great reasons to visit *www.tipsdigest.com* today:

❖ Registration to join the *Tipster Nation!* is free.

❖ You'll receive unlimited access to self-help and how-to articles (laced with our unique brand of humor, of course!), great TipBits, awesome contests and money-saving promotions.

❖ You'll receive terrific pre-publication offers on new *Tipping Points Digest* titles.

❖ You can sign up for *TipsMail*, our free, monthly e-mail newsletter featuring fantastic tips, excerpts from upcoming digest titles, special promotions and other must-have info not found anywhere else.

Four great reasons to take a long, cool sip of
www.tipsdigest.com today!

Blow Your Bank Wad:
More Than 101 Scandalous Ways to
Squander Your Kids' Inheritance

Give the liberating benefits of the SKI-ing philosophy to someone you love! We guarantee they'll be laughing all the way to the ATM!
Please rush me _____ copies of *Blow Your Bank Wad* at U.S. $13.00/ Cdn $15.00 each (price includes shipping and taxes).

You Won't Get Fooled Again:
More Than 101 Brilliant Ways to Bust *Any*
Bald-Faced Liar (Even If the Liar is Lying Beside You!)

The perfect roadmap for finding the truth, whether you're navigating a crucial business deal, interviewing job candidates with suspicious resumes, hunting for a previously enjoyed vehicle, grilling your teenager over last night's keg party, or traveling with your partner down the long highway of togetherness!
Please rush me _____ copies of *You Won't Get Fooled Again* at U.S. $13.00/Cdn $16.00 each (price includes shipping and taxes).
I have enclosed a check made payable to The FingerTip Press in the amount of $_____
[ ] U.S. [ ] Cdn (please check one)

Full Name:_____

Address: _____

City: _____ State/Province: _____

Zip/Postal Code:_____

Telephone (including area code): _____

E-Mail: _____

Please allow 3–4 weeks for delivery.

Mail to:

The FingerTip Press
14 Chestnut Street, Suite 104
St. Thomas, ON N5R 2A7
Canada